The
150
Most
Profitable
Home
Businesses
for Women

by
Katina Z. Jones

ADAMS MEDIA CORPORATION
Holbrook, Massachusetts

Published by Adams Media Corporation
260 Center Street, Holbrook, MA 02343. U.S.A.

ISBN: 1-58062-299-2

Printed in the United States of America.

J I H G F E D C B A

Library of Congress Cataloging-in-Publication Data
Jones, Katina.
150 most profitable home businesses for women / by Katina Jones.
p.   cm.
ISBN 1-58062-299-2
1. Home-based businesses. 2. New business enterprises.
3. Women-owned business enterprises—Management. 4. Businesswomen.
5. Small business—Management. 6. Success in business. I. Title: One hundred fifty most
profitable businesses for women. II. Title: Most profitable businesses for women.
III. Title.
HD2333 .J66 2000
658'.041—dc21
99-058541

Cover photo by Vincent Besnault.

This book is available at quantity discounts for bulk purchases.
For information, call 1-800-872-5627.

Visit our exciting Web site at www.businesstown.com

Contents

....

Introduction

Women's home-based businesses are flourishing. Whether the owners are salaried professionals earning extra money in their spare time, at-home moms determined to add to the family income, recent graduates paying off tuition loans, or retired women looking to make some money from a hobby, women all across the country are starting their own businesses. And no wonder! It's never been easier or more exciting to start a home-based business, and millions of us are caught up in the entrepreneurial spirit. In fact, home-based businesses currently provide full or part-time employment for more than 14 million women.

There are many good reasons for this boom. Changes in government programs since the Women's Business Ownership Act of 1988 have made it significantly easier for women to start and operate new businesses. The Small Business Administration has been a crucial resource, as it provides a strong support network through their business development centers in every state. The SBA has also helped women secure billions of dollars in start-up loans ($1.445 billion in 1995 alone!).

Aside from government programs, new technology in both the communications and the computer industries has made the ability to work from home a reality for those who want to care for their children, avoid the hectic pace of commuting, and enjoy the freedom that working from home allows.

The home business opportunities that have been selected for this book were chosen for two reasons: they could start from hobbies, interests, or skills you already have, and they have high earning potential. Take time to read through all of the business. opportunities. You'll find that there is a broad range of job descriptions and time commitments that can be done individually, or you might want to combine two businesses. There are ideas for jobs you can squeeze into your Saturday morning routines, all along the continuum to those that would involve active, forty-hour involvement with clients.

As you read through the book, you'll see that each entry begins with a quick summary of the business's vital statistics: what skills you'll need, the capital requirement necessary to get the business started, what's involved in running it, and most importantly, how much money it can yield. Here's a breakdown of what these statistics will tell you:

Start-up costs: These costs are calculated by adding together all equipment, advertising, and operating costs. We have tried to consider every possible cost, and then asked the question: "What's the least amount of money you would need to start the business the right way?"

Potential earnings: This range is calculated by multiplying typical fees by a 40-hour work week. Bear in mind that this amount can change dramatically in proportion to how much time you're able to devote to the work.

Typical fees: Each business idea has been thoroughly researched to find out what people who are actually in the business are charging their clients. For many entries, you might see a range instead of a flat fee. Your geographic location may influence your pricing strategy and the range of fees reflects this.

Advertising: Here, we have listed all the possible ways you could promote your business, from methods that cost nothing, such as networking, to developing actual media campaigns that might cost thousands of dollars a year. These costs have been figured into the actual start-up cost.

Qualifications: This category contains everything you need to know about professional certifications, personality requirements, and other information pertinent to what it takes to enter a particular field.

Equipment needed: The equipment purchases you are likely to need in order to make your business run efficiently.

Staff required: A high percentage of these businesses won't require anyone but yourself, but those needing additional staff are identified, often with a suggested number of employees.

Handicapped opportunity: You'll find that many home-based businesses are accessible to those with physical or developmental handicaps.

Hidden costs: This is probably the most important element of each entry. The costs that you don't think about are the ones to be most careful about! Many of these are costs you simply can't predict—or might not have realized are incurred by state and federal government requirements. Some may be as simple as the cost of additional gasoline.

Each entry also provides a comprehensive guide to the individual businesses. You'll get a total picture of what is involved in successfully running the kind of business that matches your skills. This section is divided into three parts:

Lowdown: Here we supply the details of exactly what each business demands of its owner, what your daily activities will be, and who your customers are. This section also includes information on specific marketing opportunities.

Start-up: You'll find an in-depth breakdown of your start-up costs, including everything from office furniture and computer equipment to advertising costs. You can also find valuable information on how to achieve specific earnings goals for each business.

Bottom Line Advice: This section points out the positive and negative aspects of each business, so you'll know exactly what you're in for. Remember, there are positives and negatives for every opportunity.

Whatever your financial incentive, starting a home-based business is a great way to earn money and be your own boss. All you need is to pick one good idea!

Part I

Putting Your Business Together

Legal Issues for Small Businesses

Many start-up businesses do not have a lawyer, and some companies operate for years without ever needing legal advice. The owners have done their homework and understand the legal situations likely to arise in their area of business. They know the government rules and regulations affecting them and have set up systems to assure that they dot the i's and cross the t's consistently, keeping accurate records to prove it.

Do You Need a Lawyer?

Generally speaking, though, entrepreneurs find that working with an attorney who specializes in small business issues saves them time, worry, and (possibly) large sums of money over the long run. This should be one of the "business advisor" relationships that strengthens your organization rather than drains its resources. You will definitely need to work with an attorney:

- If you decide to incorporate or form a partnership.
- When you need to sign a contract or agreement—understanding the legal language so you know exactly what you are committing your business to do.
- Whenever you prepare a contract or agreement for others to sign.
- If someone sues you.

Finding an Attorney

To find a good attorney, ask friends and business associates for recommendations. It is important to check each lawyer's business experience and learn about his or her general approach. You want direct, no-frills service that provides substance at the least possible cost. You need a real relationship—someone who responds to your calls within a reasonable time period, answers your questions in plain English, and takes an active interest in your business success. Most attorneys provide an initial consultation at no charge. Ask about fees. Once you have chosen your lawyer, develop a fee or retainer plan that fits your budget.

Finding a compatible attorney can be a somewhat lengthy process, and it is much better to do this before the crisis hits. In fact, good legal advice can be the stitch in time that saves you from tedious, expensive trouble later on. What is your exposure to lawsuits? If the danger is high, you might also consider insuring your business against legal costs.

Avoiding Legal Trouble

Most businesses never incur these costs, and clearly you want to do everything you can to be in that category. Set your business up and conduct it with the aim of keeping legal troubles from arising. Get business agreements in writing, and maintain clear, organized records of each transaction. Add to the files your notes on what is said in any additional telephone calls or meetings that discuss expectations, promises, modifications, and other issues.

Follow laws and regulations, those that apply generally to businesses, and those that apply to your specific business type. Make sure your employees and customers know what your policies are, and follow them yourself. This is an area where your leadership will have a more powerful effect than all the memos and employee handbooks in the world. When you do what you promise and follow through immediately to resolve complaints, you set up an atmosphere of trust. That's the best legal protection your business can have.

Agreements

New business owners may not recognize situations that actually involve an agreement or contract, even though no official piece of paper has been written to label them as such. Do you get paid in advance for a service or product to be delivered later? Do you send payment to a supplier and receive delivery of the materials later? These are really agreements: money is exchanged on the expectation that the desired result will occur.

Many slightly more experienced business owners discover a painful truth: agreements aren't always honored by the other party. You may provide a service, an expensive service that involves buying the paper to produce a catalog, hiring an associate, or accumulating travel costs. You intend to send a bill when the job is complete, but the client wants one small change after another. You finally send the bill— but it never gets paid. Unless you have excellent records of what was asked for and what you promised, as well as what you delivered, you may have no way of recovering this loss. One situation like this can destroy a fledgling business. For safety's sake, check with your attorney to set up a formal agreement procedure before your fingers get burned.

Contracts

If contracts are part of your business, you will also need to work with your attorney, to protect yourself. Getting the requests, plans, and promises down on paper is actually a good selling technique: your customer knows exactly what to expect, and you have a checklist to make sure that you perform the work to expectations. Then there will be no gray areas that could lead to discomfort, disagreements, and disappointment later.

You are protecting your business, and you are guaranteeing customer satisfaction as well. It's a win/win activity.

Contracts tend to be more formal than agreements. If you write your own, have your attorney create the first one and check any major variations that occur in later versions. If you are asked to sign a contract prepared by another organization, READ ALL OF IT. Have your attorney read it too, and explain the murky parts to you. Again, you can't provide customer satisfaction if you don't know what you're supposed to do. Renegotiate whatever provisions you do not wish to meet. The other party has the option of doing this as well. Carrying out this process in a positive manner can be a key to selling successfully. You're simply working toward a situation of mutual benefit: providing your products or services to meet their needs in a mutually agreeable way.

Copyrights

Copyrights and trademarks are methods of protecting your rights to "intellectual property," that is, ideas, words, names, and so on. The two types of protection are very different in ease of use, and they have different effects. Additionally, neither is a guarantee of anything. They simply give you the right to try to enforce your ownership. Major legal cases involving copyright infringement occasionally receive national attention in the news media, but the day-to-day application of copyright and trademark protection is extremely complex.

The copyright symbol is familiar to almost everyone. You can simply apply it yourself to the beginning of a literary, musical, dramatic, choreographic, or visual work you have created. Typically, a copyright claim takes this form: Copyright © 2000 by Mary Smith. You can't copyright an idea or a title, but you can use a claim to protect an article, photograph, painting, record, or tape. The copyright gives the creator the sole right to copy or reproduce a work. Registering a copyright with the federal government costs $30. This is an additional step, not a requirement.

Anyone who works with business material knows, however, that copyrights are infringed regularly. Intentionally or otherwise, people steal or "borrow" others' work. It's a frustrating situation, and there is no squad of government enforcers riding out from Washington, D.C., in defense of the injured parties. Definitely claim any copyright you deserve, but realize that you'll have to enforce it yourself. It can be hard to identify what is original, what is a slight alteration of your work, and what is simply material that is "common knowledge" and should not be considered original at all.

Trademarks

Trademarks apply specifically to business situations. You trademark your business name, product name, symbol, or combination of symbol and name so that no other organization can use it. The reputation for quality and service attached to your business name is protected in this way from use by sleazeballs who want to ride on your coattails.

Registering a trademark is essential, and the process is complex enough to require the assistance of an attorney who specializes in this area. An extensive search is necessary first to be sure that no one else has used "General Motors" as the name for their car company. Given the size and dynamics of the U.S. economy, it can be quite difficult to create a business name that is not already in use. Another purpose of the national trademark search, therefore, is to avoid unintentionally infringing the trademark of an established business.

Again, there is no guarantee that a trademark will protect you, but it will help prevent accidental use by another organization of your name. And it will at least discourage copycatting. To some extent, your name conveys the value and quality of your business. Your customers find you by your name, and they use your name to spread the good word to others about the value of what you provide. Your business or product name is far more, then, than just a phrase to print on your business card. Trademarking helps protect this symbol of your enterprise.

Putting Together a Solid Business Plan

A business plan is a detailed document that describes the vital elements of your enterprise, outlines the basic assumptions you are making as you develop the organization, and details your financial projections. The plan establishes your goals: what are you trying to achieve?; what specific steps will you take to achieve these goals?; what resources will be required? A well-thought-out, well-written plan is essential for gaining funding from banks and other investors. More importantly, though, producing the plan forces you to think through your business concept in a systematic way.

The plan is also a living document. Every six months, you should take the opportunity to reassess the effectiveness of the strategy you have laid out in the plan. How accurate were your assumptions? What do you now know that you can use to help the business?

Business plans can vary depending on the type of business, what is customary in a geographic area, and the specific audience. If you are submitting your plan to a bank, obtain a model plan from the loan officer for guidance. Read as many other plans as you can, and work with your business advisors as you write. Keep your readers in mind, and be sure to address their concerns. Do not assume that your readers will be familiar with the jargon and technical terminology of your business. Above all, state the assumptions behind your financial projections. Offer evidence to support each claim you make. Why is your market attractive? What information supports your projected sales figures for each of the next five years? How have you calculated your materials costs?

All business plans include these basic elements: an executive summary, a company profile, a product or service analysis, a market analysis, a marketing plan, a financial analysis, and a description of your management team.

Executive Summary

The executive summary is critical because most investors will read it first to gain a sense of your business as a whole. (Write it last, after all the details have been worked out.) Within a few pages, you should:

- Define your company and describe the management team—their expertise, management ability, and experience with start-up businesses.
- Outline your products or services and highlight the benefits they provide to your target market.
- Show evidence that your product or service is accepted by your market.

- Describe your target market.
- Analyze your competition.
- Summarize your financial prospects.
- State the amount of money you need.
- Show how the money will be used.
- Explain why your business will be successful.

Company Profile

This section describes your planned company in detail. It outlines the products, markets, and history of the business. The goal of this section is to convince your readers that you are able to produce the results that you are projecting. Here is where you establish your competitive edge—the factors that make you stand out above the competition and appeal to your target market. This section also contains your general, long-term business goals.

Product or Service Analysis

This section establishes exactly why and how your product or service is different from what is already available from other businesses. What are you offering that your target market can obtain in no other way? The features of your product are important, but what you must clarify here are the benefits.

- Outline the resources you will need to deliver the product or service: raw materials, skilled technicians, packaging, office space, etc. Discuss availability and cost.
- Describe your facility and delivery methods, equipment needed, utility costs, and other factors in the day-to-day operations of the business. Transportation, suppliers, and manufacturing issues must be outlined here.
- Explain why your product or service is unique. What value will it add to your customers' lives? Is your technology legally protected? How will you keep what you offer up to date?

Market Analysis

A market analysis supports all successful businesses and requires a great deal of research. Use the library, local trade associations, and business groups such as the Chamber of Commerce for data. The point is to illustrate the potential demand for your specific product or service. What needs are currently not being met, and why? What trends affect your market area? What changes are occurring in the business climate?

Describe your competition, what they offer, what segment they appeal to, and the reasons why their customers buy from them. Describe your likely customers: number, demographics, trends, location. Clarify the pluses and minuses of your products versus those of your competition: price, quality, appeal to the market.

Marketing Plan

The marketing plan shows how you will reach your target market. How will those who need your product or service come to understand that it is available from your business? This plan covers pricing, and the relationship of these prices to similar products and to the competition. It covers distribution, delivery, returns, and replacements.

You will outline your plans for the sales process and the methods of payment you will accept. You will describe your promotions and advertising approaches. Most importantly, you will project your sales month by month for the first year and, in general, for the four years after that.

Financial Analysis

Investors with a serious interest in your business will read this section in detail. It's the heart of your business plan. The financial analysis describes where the money will come from and how it will be spent, with projections of cash flow, income, and debt. This section includes:

- A balance sheet, a snapshot of your company's assets, liabilities, and net worth;
- An income statement, comparing your revenues and expenses over a specific period of time to show your net profit or loss;
- Projected income statement, which estimates income and expenses at a future period;
- Projected cash flow, which shows how you will manage the most difficult problem for many businesses: spending and collecting cash;
- A break-even point, the date at which your company will begin to make a profit!

Management and Advisory Team

You need to explain how your company is organized and who fills each role. Outline the responsibilities planned for each position. Some plans place the background information on each member of the management team in this section, while others put detailed resumes in an appendix.

Include enough details on key people to allow a background check. Describe their experience and highlight the strengths they bring to your specific business. Describe what each person has invested in the business and their compensation plans. Include here the names of outside owners and such business advisors as your attorney, your accountant, and other people important to the enterprise.

Why Some Start-ups Fail (and What You Can Do to Survive)

It has been said that some 60 percent of new businesses fail within their first five years. How can you protect yourself when you think you're hitting hard times?

Primary Reasons Businesses Fail:

■ Undercapitalization. You don't have enough to pay the bills and keep the creditors off your back. The phone is ringing, but you hate to answer it because it's more likely a creditor than a customer. The problem is, you're spending more than you're actually earning.

■ Poor Leadership/Direction. Your staff (if you have one) is running around in circles, and nothing seems to get accomplished. You spin your own wheels trying to assess blame rather than solve the problem. Maybe you just weren't trained to be a good manager; get training *now*.

■ Shaky Business Plan. Remember that all-important document you were supposed to work on—the one that answered all the questions about where your money would come from and how you would keep it rolling in? Maybe it's time for a look back; such time-travel can often provide important clues to what's happening and what's not in your business. But, then, you should have been looking back and updating your business plan every few months or so anyway, right?

■ Miscalculated Market Potential. Your marketing strategy should have pointed out all of your areas of opportunity, but what if you were flat wrong? What if your idea was a good one for New York City but not for Boise, Idaho? Let's face it: when we're first working on our marketing plan, we're always overly optimistic. That's why it's a good idea to have other (more cynical and objective) people look over your marketing data; they'll play devil's advocate, and you'll thank them for it later.

■ Ineffective Marketing. You've spent tons of money on advertising and wonder why it isn't paying off. Could it be that you were advertising in the wrong place—or, worse yet, to the wrong people? Once you've committed advertising budget to one or more media, you'll have a hard time pulling the dollars out when you get no response. Test your markets, and don't commit to long-term contracts until you've gotten at least a 15 percent return on three consecutive ads.

Primary Strategies for Survival:

■ Take a hard look at your debt. Too many of us shy away from what we fear most. Have the courage to get it all out into the open—and, if you don't have any courage left, call a professional bookkeeper who can help put everything in the right column again.

■ Work out alternative payment plans where you can. Often, all you'll need to do is tell your creditors you're thinking of filing bankruptcy. The word alone makes them jump at accepting payments that are significantly less than they would have gotten (to them, some money will be better than no money).

■ Sell whatever you can, if you can. If you've got equipment that's worth something, put it on the market as soon as you can. If it's critical to your business, you obviously can't sell it; if it's a piece that you could just as easily lease, it could bring in the money you need.

■ Don't think of expansion as the answer. Too many entrepreneurs think that if one aspect of their business isn't working, they should add another (rather than sub-tract the one that's not working). Don't make the mistake of growing bigger to avoid problems; you're only distracting yourself from the real issue at hand.

■ Cut expenses across the board. Some entrepreneurs get narrow-minded about controlling expenses; you'll lose your business for sure if you're not flex-ible in where you can save money.

■ Consider the worst thing that could happen. In your survival plan, you'll need to picture the most terrible thing that can happen in order to be able to work back to the most positive. Know it, face it, then work your plan.

■ Keep a positive attitude. It's hard to remain positive when you feel as though you're losing control of your business, but you need to remember that *all* businesses go through trying times. Moreover, you'll need to be positive for your employees and your customers, so that they don't lose faith in you during what might wind up being only a temporary problem.

Writing Grant Proposals and Loan Applications

Applying for a grant or loan requires much the same thinking process you went through in preparing your business plan. The reason is the same: you are presenting the facts and assumptions about your new venture to an outsider for the purpose of gaining financial resources.

A business development grant may be available to you if you are a member of a special group, depending on the state you live in. Subsidized loans may also be a pos-sibility. Women and minority business owners should make special efforts to discover what financial support programs are available to them. Most of these are administered at the state level.

The persistence that has allowed you to develop a business concept and get it off the drawing board needs to be applied to the process of seeking a grant or loan as well. You will probably have to ask many, many people before you find the right door to open, the right office to call in your state government, and the helpful person who can finally assist you with your search. A professor at a local business college may know where to guide you. A women's business group could offer assistance. Try calling the office of your state representative. Consult your library for resource guides.

A loan could be all you need to start you on the road to success, and a grant, which need not be paid back, would be an even bigger boost!

Tips on filling out the proposal or application:

- Make sure your business plan does an outstanding job of presenting your concept, marketing approach, and financial projections.
- Follow the loan or grant guidelines to the letter. If possible, obtain a model application and study it carefully.
- Have your business advisors check your completed application.

Include all required elements:

- Credit request (the amount of money needed, its intended use, and the plans for paying it back if a loan).
- A copy of your business plan.
- Federal Income Tax returns, for the last three years, for all significant members of the management team and the business owners.
- Cash flow projected similarly.
- Your projected income statement, monthly for a year and quarterly for the following three years.
- Specifics on all business debt.
- Resumes for significant participants in the enterprise.
- Source of equity, describing the contribution of each significant business backer.
- Other requirements as needed depending on the business type (construction contract for a building business) or loan type (SBA Compensation Agreement, etc.).

Marketing on a Shoestring

Whatever business you enter, you must do marketing. The people who need your product or service must be able to reach you. Take every route you can to communicate your message to prospective customers. That does not mean pouring money into untested ad campaigns or producing expensive giveaways. Creativity is much more important than money in marketing a new venture. Your ideas and commitment to the value of your product or service are the central factors in marketing success.

The first step to successful marketing is self-analysis. What are you really selling? What are the values of your business? What makes you different from similar companies? What do you offer that your customers can't do without, and can't get anywhere else? It can be difficult to come right out and tell people the answers to these questions—but you and everyone else in your organization must learn to say in one sentence what your business offers.

Advertising is only a small piece of the marketing puzzle, and some businesses thrive without ever doing it. Others use one or another type of advertising exclusively, but they go through a process of discovery first. What works well? Any cost is too much if it does not result in sales. Experiment, tracking results carefully. Repeat only those methods that work. Otherwise you will go broke fast.

An effective marketing plan is essential. Work with it for a year, and reassess. Do not neglect some of the proven techniques for marketing that cost very little and serve to make your name known in your community.

- Cooperate with other businesses—consider a joint promotion (for fitness classes and nutrition counseling, as an example).
- Be an expert—give speeches before community groups, write articles on topics related to your service offerings, etc.
- Participate in trade shows—with careful planning, you can gain follow-up opportunities, do many product demonstrations, and make contacts with prospects.
- Gain free media exposure—get publicity at no cost, receive third-party presentation for your story.
- Consider direct mail—guided by an expert, you can create an effective mailing list to reach your target market.
- Become involved in your community—genuine public service on boards and committees enhances your reputation, makes friends for your business, and gets your name out.
- Publish a newsletter quarterly—include information of interest to your target market, appealing graphics, and a focus on one of your products or services

Part II

....

150 Profitable Home Businesses

Abstracting Service

Start-up cost:	$2,500-$8,000
Potential earnings:	$20,000-$40,000 per year
Typical fees:	At least $5-$15 per article (full abstract with index)
Advertising:	Solicit database publishers, corporations, respond to newspaper ads for abstract work
Qualifications:	Knowledge in the areas you are abstracting, ability to research a wide range of topics, ability to organize and consolidate data, good writing and communication skills, knowledge of database services and CD-ROM publishers
Equipment needed:	Computer and modem, fax, printer, software, office furniture, business cards, letterhead, reference books, dictionaries
Staff required:	No
Handicapped opportunity:	Yes
Hidden costs:	Keep an eye on on-line time if using these services

Lowdown:

Abstracters read articles from various publications, summarize them, and store the data on a computer. Some abstracters also index the articles by key words or terms that help the computer locate them quickly. Often abstracters specialize in areas such as engineering, science, and other technical fields; some work in medical and legal fields. A keen interest in reading is very important to your success, as is the ability to retain what you read. Good writing skills and knowledge of the topics you are abstracting is essential, especially for condensing the material. This business could also fit well with an existing editorial services or technical writing business. If you don't have actual paid experience as an abstracter, you can select articles of interest to certain potential clients, make up a portfolio of samples, and pitch your services to them. You might also talk with database publishers to discuss how you might help them, and vice versa.

Start-up:

In addition to basic computer equipment and a word-processing package, you don't need much beyond office furniture and reference books. Your business can be launched for as little as $2,500. Charge $5-$15 per article.

Bottom Line Advice:

Many larger corporations, in particular, rely on abstracting services to keep them updated about competitors and innovations in products and services relating to their businesses. This work allows considerable flexibility in your schedule and requires only a modest investment. Abstracting demands great concentration and careful organization, but also exposes you to a wealth of knowledge and contacts. You also will have the satisfaction of knowing that your work provides a valuable service to your clients.

Adoption Search Service

Start-up cost:	$2,000-$3,000
Potential earnings:	$25,000-$40,000
Typical fees:	$150-$250 per job or an hourly fee of $15-$25 per hour
Advertising:	Yellow Pages, referrals from social service agencies and associations
Qualifications:	Experience with the field, sensitivity, understanding of state laws, rules, and records regarding adoption, persistence
Equipment needed:	Computer, modem, printer, office furniture, business cards, letterhead, envelopes
Staff required:	No
Handicapped opportunity:	Yes
Hidden costs:	On-line time, phone bills

Lowdown:

Adoption search services provide opportunities for birth children or birth parents to retrace the steps that separated them from their blood relatives. This is a challenging business, and it is still encircled with complex regulations that vary from state to state. Another source of challenge is the infinite variation of human nature. Some reunions are filled with joy, but not all discoveries are happy ones and some people would rather not be found. A vocal minority of the population strongly opposes the adoption search process. Overall, however, bridging the chasm caused by adoption decisions can be a viable service for a small business to offer.

Start-up:

Some of the searching process may be done on-line (spend $2,000-$3,000 for a computer), but the telephone and shoe leather will be your major tools. You may opt to charge a flat rate ($150-$250) or an hourly fee of $15-$25 per hour. If the client has some information for you to go on, opt for the flat rate. If it looks like a wild-goose chase, you might seriously consider the hourly rate plus related expenses.

Bottom Line Advice:

Marketing will be a challenge. How will adoptees and birth parents come to know about your service? And since you will only work once for each client, marketing must be an ongoing part of your strategy. Linking people can heal old and painful wounds, so you will get more than monetary rewards from your successful searches. On the other hand, it could throw salt into a wound that was somewhat healed. How will turning someone's life around, for good or ill, affect you?

Animal Registration/ID Services

Start-up cost:	$500-$1,000
Potential earnings:	$15,000-$30,000
Typical fees:	$6-$10 per license, $20-$40 for electronic ID service
Advertising:	Yellow Pages, veterinarians' offices, local trade fairs, word of mouth
Qualifications:	You may need to apply for a license to sell dog licenses
Equipment needed:	Electronic ID patches, computer, dog tags/licenses
Staff required:	No
Handicapped opportunity:	Yes
Hidden costs:	Insurance

Lowdown:

Pet registries contain photos and identifying information about household pets, primarily in case an animal gets lost or stolen. This information can be matched with descriptions from the Humane Society, police departments, local animal shelters, and even classified ads. Your job will be to maintain these records and conduct a little bit of a search through these channels if Fido's missing in action. You can start this business by selling dog licenses and work up to peddling the ID products as an add-on service. You will be providing a service that is as valuable to animal lovers as their pets—and that kind of loyalty can go a long way in your bank account. To really maximize your potential, you could try networking with veterinarians (who might help you via referral or by simply letting you post flyers in their offices).

Start-up:

You can launch this one without much hassle—and with as little as $500 (mostly to cover a small product inventory). Charging $6-$10 per license and $20-$40 for electronic ID products (which must be inserted by a veterinarian), you could make anywhere from $15,000-$30,000. That's not too shabby, especially if you offer this service as an add-on to an existing business (such as a hardware store, for example).

Bottom Line Advice:

People are just plain crazy about their pets, and they can be easily convinced that your products are of value to them. However, you'll need to make sure that you have a genuine interest in their animals, or it'll show.

Apartment Preparation Service

Start-up cost:	$500
Potential earnings:	$20,000–$30,000
Typical fees:	$50 and up per apartment
Advertising:	Yellow pages, direct contact with apartment owners
Qualifications:	Knowledge of cleaning procedures and painting skills
Equipment needed:	Cleaning supplies, sweeper, mops, buckets, painting equipment
Staff required:	No
Handicapped opportunity:	No
Hidden costs:	Insurance, equipment maintenance

Lowdown:

You add the finishing touches to apartment buildings before the next tenant moves in. To increase your marketability, offer several services, including carpet cleaning, wall washing, painting and wallpaper repair, and overall cleaning services. Set fee schedules appropriately depending on individual services (or offer an all-inclusive package price). Advertise your services to many apartment complexes. To cut down on driving, try to get a contract with a multi-unit apartment complex offering short-term lease options.

Start-up:

Invest in good quality cleaning equipment, including a sweeper and carpet cleaner. Start-up costs can be as low or as high as you want, depending on what services you are going to offer and the quality of equipment you purchase. This business can be started for a relatively low cost with high return on investment.

Bottom Line Advice:

This business is not for someone who is afraid of good hard elbow grease. Be prepared to encounter some messy situations. An apartment preparer might spend quite a bit of time on her hands and knees cleaning baseboards and floors—consider the health of your back and always wear a back corset. In addition, invest in a good pair of knee pads and rubber gloves.

Arts Festival Promoter

Start-up cost:	$500-$1,000
Potential earnings:	$20,000-$45,000+
Typical fees:	40 percent of registration fees from artists; often, you'll also make a commission from each ticket sold
Advertising:	Word of mouth, ads in artists' newsletters and publications, direct mail to artists, newspaper/billboard ads for the event itself
Qualifications:	Strong organizational skills
Equipment needed:	Computer with desktop publishing software and laser printer
Staff required:	No (you can solicit volunteers to work at each festival)
Handicapped opportunity:	Possibly
Hidden costs:	Insurance and low attendance due to poor advertising or inclement weather

Lowdown:

Annual arts festivals abound in nearly every community, and you could cash in on the public's interest in the arts by sponsoring or promoting your own group of arts festivals. Give your events a flashy name so that you can win instant recognition with your buying public and among artists (who get barraged with requests to appear in shows all over the country). You'll need to promote your festivals two ways: first, to artists who might like to participate; second, to folks who might like to attend. So, your advertising budget must be split to cater to both "customers." Set your festivals apart somehow by inviting only particular types of artists/crafters or by attaching your festivals to some sort of theme (such as an Oktoberfest arts festival). That way, you've set an annual time for the show to be expected to recur; build your mailing list for the following year by requiring everyone to sign in (or, better yet, by offering a drawing for an exquisite work of art).

Start-up:

You'll need $500-$1,000 to launch this interesting and artistic enterprise; this seed money will primarily cover your computer costs (printer, desktop publishing software) and a little advertising until you've got one or two shows under your belt. Once you've established a name for your arts festivals, you could have annual repeat business in certain areas and begin to make more than $45,000 per year doing something you truly enjoy.

Bottom Line Advice:

You love the arts, and know that others like artsy events. So what's the downside? The only real negative is that sometimes the weather rains on your parade of artists. You could avoid such mishaps if you hold all of your events indoors; even though it may raise your space rental cost, the payoff might be worth it.

Expert Advice

Myra Mayman
Arts Festival Promoter

On Planning an Event

In my field, every event requires the tedious, nuts-and-bolts work of setting things up—the planning process. Early on, you have to schedule the meetings, send out memos to get people to the meetings, and have your databases updated, so that when the time comes to put on an event, you can contact people from a list without additional research. For every one-weekend event, there's a lot of preparation work going on throughout the year.

A good way to get into this business is to have some experience doing smaller-scale productions—anything from special events at institutions, to producing a play, to putting on a concert. You might also gain relevant experience by being a community activist—a person who gets people together and makes something happen. In general, you need to be a person who can cope with adrenaline rushes and crisis management—all that is part of putting on a show.

Association Management Services

Start-up cost:	$2,000-$9,000
Potential earnings:	$20,000-$50,000
Typical fees:	Monthly retainers of $1,000-$5,000 are not uncommon (directly dependent upon the association's size)
Advertising:	Network with professional and trade associations, advertise in related publications
Qualifications:	Good organizational, writing, marketing, communication, and motivation skills, an eye for detail, office management or administrative experience is helpful
Equipment needed:	Office and computer equipment, phone, fax, copier, business cards, letterhead, supplies
Staff required:	No
Handicapped opportunity:	Yes
Hidden costs:	Membership in associations; subscriptions to related publications

Lowdown:

From the Association for Association Management (yes, there really is an association for everyone) to the Association for Children for Enforcement of Support, most organizations need help in managing their operations. Especially well-suited to a management service are groups too big to rely solely on volunteers but not big enough to justify hiring someone to do it on a full-time basis. Your services for each client may vary, but may include maintaining membership lists, publishing a newsletter, mailing out information about the organization, keeping records, collecting dues, and handling meetings, events, and fund-raising activities. Not only can you work for an existing organization, you could also start an association of your own. Best bet: base it on your own profession or something else with which you have personal experience.

Start-up:

Office and computer equipment are your biggest expenses (about $2,000). You may be able to get the organization(s) you represent to pay for some supplies, but that is not something to rely on at the business plan stage. Charge a monthly retainer of $1,000-$5,000 for your services to make sure you cover all of your expenses; since many of these associations work with volunteers, they may try to take advantage of your expertise, too. Don't let them.

Bottom Line Advice:

Association management provides a great variety of duties and an opportunity to interact with interesting people. You will also get opportunities to learn about an array of topics at meetings and conventions. This is a great opportunity for those with philanthropic tendencies.

Advertising Effectively— and Economically

You've started a business and you need to get the word out. The problem is, you simply don't have the kind of budget that Martha Stewart Living Omnimedia, LLC has to advertise your products or services. What can you do? You could try one or more of these economical methods:

- **Press releases.** Free press is the best, when you are lucky enough to get it. Try to offer tips to a particular group of people, and you'll have a better chance of catching the interest of an editor.
- **Flyers.** Post them everywhere your potential customers go. If you've got a moving or packing service, a flyer strategically located at a laundromat or apartment complex bulletin board might yield some quick results for you. Be where they are, and you'll go far.
- **Get an Internet address, or design a Web page.** The advertising wave of the future is on the 'Net. Why? Because it is so inexpensive compared to print media. Will it help you get all the business you need? That remains to be seen, but all indications are good. One pie baker sold a thousand pies the first few months after she posted her Web site. If she can do that, imagine what you could do.
- **Offer coupon deals regularly.** Coupons are ads that come with souvenirs for your customers; you get the sale, they walk away with a prize for doing business with you: a lower price or a better deal. Who can beat that?
- **Trades for advertising space.** Often, you might have a service that a local newspaper or TV/radio station needs. You can sometimes trade your services for free space or airtime.
- **Direct mail.** You can spend a small amount of money and reach a large number of potentials through direct mail pieces. Be sure to design something that's interesting and captivating. Your clients are deluged with such pieces (sometimes referred to as "junk mail") so yours needs to be fairly innovative and attention-getting. Work with a professional (you can trade services here, too) to write and design your direct mail pieces.

Athletic Recruiter/Scout

Start-up cost:	$1,000
Potential earnings:	$15,000 or more
Typical fees:	$25 per hour or more
Advertising:	Networking, referrals, participation in athletic boosters clubs, attendance at games
Qualifications:	Knowledge and love of sports, enthusiasm for young people, ability to spot talent, commitment to the team or school for which you want to recruit
Equipment needed:	Car
Staff required:	No
Handicapped opportunity:	No
Hidden costs:	Transportation costs, telephone bills

Lowdown:

You do this anyway, right? Every game you go to, you notice the players who stand out, who make the great catches, who come through in the final minutes with the setup that leads to the winning score. You see the "unsung heroes" who support the stars, and you have a sense for the kids with commitment. You can turn your interests into a business by contracting with a college or professional athletic team or teams as a scout. As a recruiter, you will establish the initial contact with the player and his or her family. You will show them the opportunities that may be available for scholarships and for participation in a sports program with spirit and great coaching.

Start-up:

All you really need to do is get yourself to the games (not much more than $1,000 needed initially). If you have to write reports, a secretarial service can type them for you. Depending on how much time you put in, or if you work for colleges, $15,000 can be achievable for part-time work.

Bottom Line Advice:

You'll need to be the kind of person in whom athletic directors, coaches, players, and parents feel confident. You'll need the patience to sit through the games that lack excitement and the games that are played in bad weather. Converting yourself from a fan to a worker means losing some of the spontaneity of just watching and enjoying the contest. Instead, you'll be analyzing all the time: how is this player progressing? Who was able to spark the team to greater effort in the second half? Will this player look as good at the next level of competition? This is not a way to get rich, but it has the satisfaction of bringing out excellence and helping young people find opportunities.

Auto Paint Touch-Up Professional

Start-up cost:	$500-$1,000
Potential earnings:	$15,000-$25,000
Typical fees:	$30-$50 per job
Advertising:	Memberships and active participation at car enthusiast events, direct mail, flyers, referrals from dealers and auto repair stores, radio spots, classified ad in auto sales section of newspaper
Qualifications:	Some experience with auto paint work, sales skills
Equipment needed:	Inventory of popular paint colors, sander, brush
Staff required:	No
Handicapped opportunity:	No
Hidden costs:	Inventory and disposal of used chemicals

Lowdown:

It's not the big things that drive us crazy, sometimes, it's the dings in our car doors and the chips off the hood. For an entirely new paint job, or the replacement of a crumpled fender, plenty of sources are available in most communities. But how can people keep those little scratches and chips from slowly ruining the appearance and resale value of their cars? That's where your service comes in. You can fix the small stuff, which is important nowadays just to keep a car's body panel warranty in effect. Your business meets the need for a smaller, less expensive way to maintain the smooth surface that your customers' vehicles had when new.

Start-up:

Costs are low (about $500 for materials); your skill in doing neat-looking paint touch-ups is your main product. On a part-time basis alone you could earn in excess of $15,000.

Bottom Line Advice:

Can you find a way to combine customers? Would it work to fix the scratches in every car in the parking garage or lot of a huge company? Can you be an add-in to the work of a local detailer, car wash, or used car lot? You decide—and market yourself accordingly, perhaps offering group discounts.

Automobile Window Stickers

Start-up cost:	$5,000-$10,000
Potential earnings:	$15,000-$25,000
Typical fees:	$5-$10 per sticker
Advertising:	Networking and direct mail to car dealerships
Qualifications:	None
Equipment needed:	Mobile printer with preprinted forms
Staff required:	No
Handicapped opportunity:	Yes
Hidden costs:	Insurance, equipment maintenance

Lowdown:

The used car industry depends on having adequate information about each car on each lot, and the best way to achieve such accuracy regarding a particular auto's history is to have printed labels on each car window, detailing such critical information as mileage, special features, and life cycle of particular items such as tires and timing belts. All of this information needs to be displayed prominently on the inside driver's side window, and in a professional, standard-looking manner. After all, used car dealers base much of their sales on credibility these days, and they depend on items as seemingly unimportant as your product to build customer trust. The buying public is far too smart to be duped by "lemon" automobiles; those who don't know a lot about cars are beginning to hire automotive inspection services to check out a car before they buy it. Your main objective in this straightforward business is to sell to dealers on-site, print out the labels immediately, and collect your cash.

Start-up:

You'll need about $5,000-$10,000 to start this business well, mainly because you'll probably be buying into a franchise (unless, of course, you have access to the specialized forms and printer you'll need to produce labels). Your advertising budget can be rather small, due to the fact that your growth will be based on reputation and networking success. Expect to earn anywhere from $15,000-$25,000 as you run around from dealer to dealer, building lasting relationships based on short-term need.

Bottom Line Advice:

This is a simple business to manage and run—but you'll really need to be of immediate and accurate service to your clients to keep the cash rolling in. Any time you're not available to them, they'll use a competitor (and you know what that can do to your bank account).

Band Manager

Start-up cost:	$500-$1,000
Potential earnings:	$15,000-$25,000
Typical fees:	10 to 25 percent of a gig
Advertising:	Industry trades, local paper, direct mail, nightclubs, bulletin boards, musicians' associations
Qualifications:	An ear for what will sell, management skills
Equipment needed:	Computer, laser printer, phone, letterhead, business cards
Staff required:	No
Handicapped opportunity:	Yes
Hidden costs:	Band could fire you without notice; it might be a good idea to represent several

Lowdown:

You're into the club scene; you know instinctively what's hot and what's not. You see a few up-and-coming bands who need representation (because, truthfully, most musicians lack business skills). If you've got the ability to convince musicians that you can really sell them and make their jobs easier by handling all of the business details they'd probably rather not think of anyway, you could make a decent living. You'll need to be well-connected on the club scene, and if you are clued in on where to plug your band(s), you could successfully book them for regular gigs and earn a steady flow of income for yourself in the meantime. Of course, you need to really believe in your band, because if you don't, you won't be able to develop and promote them properly and it will show in your presentation. Good negotiation skills are a must.

Start-up:

You'll need some initial capital ($500-$1,000) to help get the band off the ground and lay the ground for some publicity. The ability to negotiate good contracts is important not only to the band, but to you because you get roughly 10 to 25 percent of what they make. With percentages like that, you could make $15,000-$25,000 (depending on how many bands you represent).

Bottom Line Advice:

Expect to spend long hours on the phone trying to get bookings. At the start, you'll probably still have a day job, so expect your evenings and weekends to be tied up. Start out at small clubs and work your way to bigger ones as your band(s) get more confident.

Bartending Services

Start-up cost:	Under $1,000
Potential earnings:	$10,000-$20,000
Typical fees:	$15-$30 per hour, or a flat per-event rate
Advertising:	Classified ads, bulletin boards, community newspapers
Qualifications:	Must be legal age (and should know how to make drinks without looking them up)
Equipment needed:	None
Staff required:	Might be a good idea to have one or two other bartenders
Handicapped opportunity:	Possibly
Hidden costs:	None apparent, so just watch your mileage

Lowdown:

Being a traveling bartender service for private parties is an exciting way to meet people and make money at the same time. You'll mix libations for everyone from wealthy executives to people at a family celebration, and the time will always pass quickly. You'll need to make sure that if you are expected to bring the beverages, you secure funds for that ahead of time to avoid excessive outlay of your own cash. Be sure to add in the cost of delivering the goods as well. The best way to get started is to produce professional-looking business cards and leave them prominently displayed at a few of your first jobs. In fact, you may want to do your first five jobs for free (if you feel you'll get a lot of attention)—that may be a great way to start the highballs rolling!

Start-up:

With virtually nothing to lose but your time, you could do far worse than start a bartending service. Invest in a few good mixology handbooks and you're off to a great start! You also may want to visit the more progressive bars in your area to see if the bartenders know of any interesting new drinks—the more you can offer your clients, the happier they will be.

Bottom Line Advice:

You'll really absorb the energy and variety of bartending work, but it can be tiring to stand on your feet in one place for too long. Remember to bring a bar stool for yourself—and invest in a good pair of shoes with soothing inserts!

Barter Systems

Start-up cost:	$500-$1,000
Potential earnings:	$15,000 and up
Typical fees:	$15 or more per transaction
Advertising:	Penny savers, community newspaper classifieds, bulletin boards, flyers, networking, participation in community activities related to recycling, cooperative grocery stores
Qualifications:	Friendliness, detail orientation
Equipment needed:	A computer would help you keep track of the information, but you could use a paper system as well
Staff required:	No
Handicapped opportunity:	Yes
Hidden costs:	Phone bill may be higher than expected

Lowdown:

You know everyone. You never waste a penny. You love to solve problems, and to help other people solve theirs. That's why you will derive great satisfaction from your barter system business. It's really just putting two and two together: what someone has, with what someone needs, and vice versa. Making it all work as a profitable business will be a bit more challenging than just this (which you have probably been doing on an amateur basis most of your life). Many barter systems are warehouse operations, with individuals buying bulk odd lots and then trying to trade them. You will need to become known, to gather the data, the offerings, and the needs, and to work continually at the matches. Creating some kind of valuation system for disparate objects and services may pose difficulties also: how does a carwash match up with a soccer ball? Trading small ski boots for larger ones is easier.

Start-up:

Costs will be minimal (only about $500 to start). You'll need some way for your clientele to reach you, and some way to track what is bartered. Your thoughtfulness is your real product in this business. A part-time business should net you around $15,000.

Bottom Line Advice:

Barter systems appeal to people who try to live inexpensively and not wastefully—the cooperative market types, people in academic communities, and creative thinkers who are trying to step off the whirl of consumerism that keeps the rest of us in debt. You'll develop repeat customers if you can help people achieve their wants, and get rid of their don't-wants, without the exchange of large sums of money—just a small fee to you for the privilege. This business is a classic example of making something out of nothing. Virtually no investment, no training required, nothing but hard work on your part.

Bed & Breakfast

Start-up cost:	$60,000 (assuming you already own building)
Potential earnings:	$35,000-$175,000
Typical fees:	$125+ per room, per night (depending on season)
Advertising:	Yellow Pages, B&B directories, direct mail to travel agencies
Qualifications:	None
Equipment needed:	Beds, towels, dining tables/chairs, stationery/brochures
Home business potential:	Yes
Staff required:	Yes (but it could be comprised of family members)
Handicapped opportunity:	Unlikely (but not impossible)
Hidden costs:	Be sure your prices cover everything from electricity to food

Lowdown:

Large verandas for after-dinner strolls . . . billowy white curtains blowing in the wind . . . quiet meals by firelight. The sheer romance of owning and operating a Victorian-style B&B inn can be intoxicating enough to entice you into starting one of your own. If marketing trends are on target, more and more folks are looking for unusual escapes from city turmoil—and what better place to recuperate than a quiet little inn in the middle of nowhere (but within close driving distance to somewhere). You'll need anywhere from two to 12 extra rooms for guest accommodations, in addition to adequate kitchen and dining space. You will need to be meticulous in your cleaning and make sure that all prepared foods follow strict regulations. Also, be sure to educate yourself on all of the tourist attractions in your immediate area—you'll be surprised how often customers will count on your local expertise in devising their travel plans.

Start-up:

You'll need at least $100,000-$400,000 if you purchase a building; you may also look into buying an existing B&B and simply taking over the business (turnover is relatively high, as many owners burn out after a period of ten years or so). If you already have a building, put aside extra cash ($5,000-$10,000) for repairs and updates, in addition to another $10,000 to cover your initial operating costs. You'll spend between $1,500-$5,000 on your first six months of advertising as well. But, considering that you'll charge clients $125 and up per night, you should be able to develop a steady cash flow within the first 5 years of your business plan's projections.

Bottom Line Advice:

You could easily be drawn in to the seemingly idyllic country inn lifestyle. But before you launder the sheets and open your doors to guests, give a lot of thought to the hard work ahead; most B&B owners will tell you that there are long hours of intense work (cooking, cleaning, and assisting guests in all of their needs). If you don't mind putting in a 60+ hour work week without the promise of grand riches, a bed & breakfast inn can be a great match.

Checklist for Success:

Can You Be a Successful Entrepreneur?
Here are some questions you might ask yourself before embarking on a new business:

- ❑ Are you unhappy with your current situation—and ready for a change?
- ❑ Are you completely self-directed; that is, able to come up with and complete your own job requirements?
- ❑ Are you able to meet with and sell to many different types of people?
- ❑ Are you an expert planner—someone who can see not only the big picture, but every tiny line that created the big picture?
- ❑ Can you set and keep deadlines?
- ❑ Are you a clock-watcher, or someone who quickly loses track of time?
- ❑ Can you commit to projects and follow them through to completion every time?
- ❑ Are you adaptable and open to learning new ways of doing things?
- ❑ Do you have the mental and physical stamina you need to run your business?
- ❑ Are you afraid of risk?
- ❑ Do you have adequate savings to cover your first year's salary?
- ❑ Are you a positive person?

Book Indexer

Start-up cost:	$500-$1,000
Potential earnings:	$15,000-$30,000
Typical fees:	$2.50-$4.00 per printed book page
Advertising:	Direct mail to book publishers, Yellow Pages, industry newsletters
Qualifications:	A strong eye for detail and subject matter; impeccable organizational skills
Equipment needed:	Computer with alphabetical sorting capability, printer
Staff required:	No
Handicapped opportunity:	Definitely
Hidden costs:	Your time—indexes are complex and time-consuming, and must be accurate

Lowdown:

When you're reading a book and you want to find information on a specific topic, you look in the index first. But it probably didn't occur to you that putting together an index is a job dependent upon painstaking accuracy and attention to detail. It's an area of specialization that sets professional indexers apart from other editorial types. These folks are typically not writers (although they can be), and they are not really editors, either. Their expertise is sought after the book is written and edited, but prior to publication; they provide readers with a service that enables them to conduct research or just locate topics of interest to them, saving them time in combing through the entire book. Obviously, indexers work with nonfiction books, but the subject matter can be extremely varied and could include everything from automotive manuals to business or self-help guides. A good place to start if you feel that your organizational skills are up to this kind of work is the American Society of Indexers in New York City. Joining organizations such as this prestigious association could instantly raise your credibility level.

Start-up:

Start-up costs are almost negligible for indexing. Begin with memberships in key organizations, then submit a letter of interest or resume to book publishers in and out of your area. Set aside at least $500-$1,000 for working capital; you may need it to furnish your office with a comfortable chair (a must). Charge anywhere from $2.50-$4.00 per printed book page; for example, a 200-page book will net you $500 minimum for your indexing work.

Bottom Line Advice:

Low initial investment makes this a win-win if you don't mind detail-oriented work. The hours may be long, the turnaround time may be quicker than you had hoped, but the ability to generate income is there for those with talent.

Bookkeeping Service

Start-up cost:	$2,000-$9,000
Potential earnings:	Typically $20,000-$50,000 per year
Typical fees:	$25-$35 per hour; more for financial statements and other tasks. Certain clients may pay a flat monthly fee rather than hourly charges
Advertising:	Ads (phone book, trade publications), networking, referrals (from CPAs, for example)
Qualifications:	Knowledge of basic bookkeeping principles, some legal and tax knowledge, ability to use a computer, accounting/spreadsheet software, good eye for detail, honesty, good communications skills
Equipment needed:	Basic computer and office equipment, a financial calculator, and accounting software
Staff required:	No
Handicapped opportunity:	Yes
Hidden costs:	Organizational dues, if applicable

Lowdown:

Small business owners, in particular, use bookkeeping services to keep up with the ever-changing tax laws and the constant flow of bookkeeping details they don't have time for. Clients need help with such tasks as making deposits, reconciliation of bank statements and preparing financial reports, payroll, billing, and accounts payable and receivable, to name a few. What's the difference between bookkeeping and accounting? Bookkeepers are the record keepers; an accountant's job is to analyze and audit the records. If you have a clear, logical mind and common sense, this may be a great business for you. It is recession-proof, essential work that can be challenging and fun.

Start-up:

The required computer and office equipment can be acquired for as little as $2,000. Add another $500 or so for your first six months of advertising, and you'll be all set. You might consider joining business owners' associations or your local Chamber of Commerce to generate business. Charges for your services will vary according to the extent of the project, but the average fees are $25-$35 per hour.

Bottom Line Advice:

This work gives you a great opportunity to learn more about the business world—and about specific fields of business. The work requires close attention to each detail and necessitates your staying current about tax-law changes relating to payroll and record keeping. Mistakes may cause problems for your clients with the government; clients may also blame you for mistakes that they made. If you like numbers and enjoy working independently to solve problems, bookkeeping may be a great career for you.

Bridal Consultant

Start-up cost:	$1,000-$3,500
Potential earnings:	$25,000-$60,000 (depending on volume and location)
Advertising:	Bridal magazines (many areas have their own local versions), bridal salons, newspapers, word of mouth
Qualifications:	An eye for detail and a cool head
Equipment needed:	Cellular phone, computer plus software for contacts and clients
Staff required:	Sometimes
Handicapped opportunity:	Yes
Hidden costs:	Keep accurate records of the time you spend with each client, or you could short-change yourself.

Lowdown:

Wedding planning can easily turn any reasonable household into a temporary war zone—and that's where bridal consultants have entered the picture. With most families spending anywhere from $10,000-$15,000 and up on the wedding extravaganza itself, what's a few extra dollars to take the headache out of the blessed event's planning? Your rates would range from $50 per hour to a flat fee of $1,000 or more for the entire wedding, so it is easy to see how you could earn a profitable amount of money in a short period of time. But don't think you won't work hard for it. As a bridal consultant, you will handle every minute detail, from the number of guests to invite to what kind of champagne to buy. You are essentially in the hotbed of the action, with total responsibility for every aspect of the wedding.

Start-up:

You will need to develop strong word of mouth (try forging reciprocal referral arrangements with florists and bridal and hair salons) to build a good reputation. Also, since this is a people- and image-oriented business, you will need to make sure you look like you're worth it; dress professionally and carry yourself with poise and an air of diplomacy. But the bulk of your start-up will be in producing business cards and brochures in addition to placing newspaper and bridal magazine ads (count on forking over at least $1,000 for those items).

Bottom Line Advice:

The flash and excitement of impending nuptials can be intoxicating, as can the power involved in directing others to perform their best. Be careful not to offend anyone or step on their toes. Listen to what your customers tell you they want—and have the good sense to make them think all of the good ideas were theirs. While such ego-suppression is hard to accomplish in a high-profile job like this one, remember that the customer is always queen.

Bridal Show Promotions

Start-up cost:	$5,000-$15,000
Potential earnings:	$20,000-$40,000
Typical fees:	$125 per booth rental space
Advertising:	Flyers, radio ads, newspapers, bridal shops, mailings, billboards
Qualifications:	Exceptional organizational skills
Equipment needed:	Computer with mailing list program
Staff required:	Not initially
Handicapped opportunity:	Possibly
Hidden costs:	Radio ads are expensive; try to secure or split costs with sponsors

Lowdown:

Bridal shows are popular in every town—there are always young women who seek the best in wedding preparations. You should have no trouble securing an audience if you book in the right places (such as shopping malls, banquet halls, and hotels). Your biggest challenge will be to gain the attention, support, and dollars from participating vendors, who could be made up of businesses like caterers, florists, musicians, and cake decorators. You must be highly organized, however, to pull this one off convincingly. Lose sight of details and you'll instantly lose credibility with your audience as well as your vendors. The best advice is to secure your financial support up front to avoid any of your own out-of-pocket expenses—that way, in the event of a no-show vendor, you'll still have your cash.

Start-up:

The $5,000-$15,000 you'll need to get this business off the ground properly will mainly cover your advertising and promotional costs. Remember that you'll need to have professional-looking materials to sell vendors on in the first place, let alone the flyers and billboards to attract your audience. Do it all correctly and you'll pull in between $20,000-$40,000 yourself, depending on how many shows you run per year.

Bottom Line Advice:

If you can't get at least 50 vendors for your first show, maybe you ought to rethink your marketing strategy. Try a novel approach, or try to get a well-known spokesperson or celebrity to appear. Do everything humanly possible to attract attention.

Bulletin Board Services

Start-up cost:	$1,000-$3,000
Potential earnings:	$5,000-$15,000
Typical fees:	Monthly subscription fees start at $10; annual are $20-$50
Advertising:	On-line services
Qualifications:	On-line marketing skills
Equipment needed:	High-power computer with fax/modem, printer, phone
Staff required:	No
Handicapped opportunity:	Yes
Hidden costs:	On-line time can get expensive

Lowdown:

In the computer age, more and more folks are seeking special places to communicate with others who have similar interests. Your online bulletin board could provide such a place. You would advertise the availability of such a bulletin board, then post as many pieces of related information as possible to generate the number of users tapping into your service. The more information you have on-line, the more you'll be able to charge individuals for getting to this data. A related service that is even more important is to check the messages frequently and remove outdated ones. You can see that messages are arranged neatly and any inappropriate material is removed on a regular basis. Check with major carriers to familiarize yourself with their bulletin board regulations—and any possible charges you may incur from them for use of their on-line services.

Start-up:

All you will really need to start is a computer with a modem (about $2,000). Bulletin boards are widely available; check carefully to avoid duplicating another service or you may have some problems. What you earn is directly dependent upon how many people use your service, so make sure your topic is of wide-ranging interest.

Bottom Line Advice:

Skills and patience are the two vital ingredients to sell here. To gain repeat business, you have to keep up with the bulletin boards under your care. A large clientele is needed to make an adequate profit overall—and remember that some competing BBs are offered for free.

Business Plan Writer/Packager

Start-up cost:	$5,000-$10,000
Potential earnings:	$30,000-$100,000
Typical fees:	$3,000-$6,000 per plan (about 2 weeks of work)
Advertising:	Teaching courses on business development, networking, business associations, referrals from bankers and entrepreneurship centers, advertising in local business newsletters
Qualifications:	Understanding of financial statements, savvy business sense, excellent oral and written communication skills, ability to get people to work together, experience writing business plans
Equipment needed:	Computer, fax/modem, laser printer, suite software, business-planning software, office furniture, business cards, letterhead, envelopes, brochures
Staff required:	No
Handicapped opportunity:	Yes
Hidden costs:	Organizational dues, business periodical and newspaper subscriptions, insurance

Lowdown:

Businesses are being created all over the country at a phenomenal rate. All of these new enterprises can get two kinds of benefits from having a business plan. First, the plan structures the efforts of everyone involved, outlining what needs to be done and describing the means by which those goals will be achieved. It highlights the feasibility of the products or services the enterprise will be marketing. Most importantly, it estimates expenses and revenues, along with projections. If the revenues won't cover the expenses, it doesn't matter what wonderful things could happen down the road. The cash-starved business won't be able to get there to achieve them.

The second benefit of having a business plan is to obtain financing. A business plan is essential for the process of obtaining bank loans and most other types of outside financing. You can take your good sense of business and finance, your high-level business writing skills, and your ability to communicate with fledgling entrepreneurs and earn a hefty annual income writing business plans.

Start-up:

The equipment and materials to present a reassuringly professional image are fairly costly (in the neighborhood of $3,000-$10,000). You'll need to be able to produce a very polished printout of the final plan, most likely using one of the better-quality business plan software packages available (about $150-$300). But, you can charge $3,000 and up for each package, with hourly fees of $45 and up (depending on your location).

Bottom Line Advice:

If you have developed the wide range of skills necessary to do this work, you undoubtedly are the kind of person who loves it and can tolerate the tedious parts. What could be more rewarding than helping a new enterprise take wing and fly? It is very difficult to write an effective business plan, but that is the very reason your market exists. Each situation is different; that means opportunities for constant learning on your part. Once you complete a plan, you will need to find another client, so your marketing must be ongoing. Some business start-ups are shaky, even sleazy, although most failures are due to poor marketing and undercapitalization rather than dishonesty. In any case, try to get at least half your fee up front. You will really be a combination counselor/consultant for the entrepreneurs.

10 Ways to Expand Your Business for Little Cash

1. **Get on the Internet.** For just a few dollars per month, you can market your services worldwide. Who can beat that?
2. **Trade services with a franchisee prospect.** You could work a deal where a potential franchisee's buy-in fee would be cut if they helped produce the operations manual; this way, you use one franchisee to get more franchisees. The payoff comes later.
3. **Hire commission-only sales reps.** You only need to pay them what they earn.
4. **Hire interns from colleges and universities.** They often work for free or next-to-nothing, and get college credit in return.
5. **Participate in business organizations where you can network for free.**
6. **Find inexpensive ways to advertise your company on a regular basis** (such as asking all family members with a car to sport your company logo).
7. **Join forces with a compatible business.** For instance, you could merge with a secretarial service if you are a resume service.
8. **Put on seminars, charging a fee for teaching others your own skills.**
9. **Sponsor trade shows or other events.**
10. **Develop a program or system for your business that can be marketed and sold to others.** You could write a book or develop a software program for mass production.

Buyer's Information Service

Start-up cost:	$3,000-$6,000
Potential earnings:	$30,000-$50,000
Typical fees:	$25 and up
Advertising:	Trade journals, local and national business periodicals, Yellow Pages, memberships in business associations and community groups, networking, referrals
Qualifications:	An understanding of and experience in the purchasing world
Equipment needed:	Office furniture, computer, high-speed modem, fax, printer, cellular phone, on-line accounts, business cards, letterhead, envelopes
Staff required:	Yes
Handicapped opportunity:	Yes
Hidden costs:	On-line account fees, utility costs

Lowdown:

A buyer's information service does the legwork for overburdened purchasing departments. Researching the features and availability of new or unusual products, parts, or materials takes a great deal of time, experience, and persistence. Outsourcing this specialized work makes sense for many organizations, and your business supplies the need. You will probably specialize in a business type (electronics manufacturing, sports retail) or in a materials area (chemicals, lumber). Having an excellent network will enable you to gather the information your clients want quickly and thoroughly.

Start-up:

Communications are vital; you'll be on the phone a lot, and the Internet will supply much of the information you need ($3,000 to start). Once you build your network, $30,000 and up should be easily attained.

Bottom Line Advice:

This business is a facet of the "information age." Yes, there's lots of information available, but finding what is needed, when it's needed, is possibly even more difficult than it was in the past. Sorting through the blizzard of product data, materials sources, prices, and requirements for the relevant facts is a real challenge. You'll need to be very persistent, detail-oriented, and focused on your clients' needs to make a success of this business. Once you become known as "the answer," you'll have a steady stream of repeat business and referrals.

Cake Decorator

Start-up cost:	$100-$200
Potential earnings:	$5,000-$25,000
Typical fees:	$10-$1,000 per cake
Advertising:	Word of mouth, newspaper ads, neighborhood bulletins
Qualifications:	Cake baking and decorating knowledge
Equipment needed:	Baking pans and utensils, decorating supplies, ingredients, oven
Staff required:	None
Handicapped opportunity:	Yes
Hidden costs:	Make sure you have enough kitchen space for finished cakes; may need a second oven or other facilities as business grows; need vehicle if you deliver

Lowdown:

People love home-baked goodies. All it takes to satisfy that need is an oven, some recipes, and a way (brochure, advertisement) to tell customers you're in business. Birthday cakes for children are especially popular; a home baker can customize and personalize them in countless ways to please the customer. Wedding cakes can be very lucrative but require more time and equipment than cakes for other occasions. Nowadays people want to choose from more than chocolate, vanilla, or yellow cakes—the sky's the limit!

Start-up:

Start-up costs for a cake-baking business are minimal. Some great recipes, baking pans, decorating supplies, utensils, and an oven (your kitchen range will do just fine) are all that you need. If you can't easily learn to decorate cakes from a book or by trial-and-error, you may want to invest in an inexpensive cake decorating course. If you plan to deliver the cakes, you will need an appropriate vehicle.

Bottom Line Advice:

The potential market out there is huge, especially since most working women and men don't have time to bake, but still want homemade cakes. There are so many special occasions to celebrate, and most of them feature great cakes: graduations, birthdays, anniversaries, retirement parties, baby and wedding showers, weddings . . . the list is endless! A cake that can be made for as little as 60 cents can sell for as much as $9— a nice profit for your efforts! On the downside, it may take some practice to make beautiful cakes. You also need patience and good marketing skills to build your business.

Calligrapher

Start-up cost:	$150-$500
Potential earnings:	$10,000-$15,000
Typical fees:	$50-$75 per invitation, other items on a per-job basis
Advertising:	Classified ads, bridal magazines, bulletin boards
Qualifications:	A steady hand and a love for lettering
Equipment needed:	Calligraphy pens and ink, parchment or specialty paper
Staff required:	No
Handicapped opportunity:	Possibly
Hidden costs:	Don't spend too much on advertising until you're sure of your market

Lowdown:

The fine art of calligraphy began in medieval times, when monks joyously and labori-ously produced biblical text using intricate, artistic lettering. This regal writing appears today in items such as wedding invitations, birth notices, and certificates of merit. You could also produce suitable-for-framing family trees (the customer would, of course, need to supply the data). Without a huge initial investment, you can offer your services to schools (for diplomas), brides-to-be (for addressing invitations), athletic teams, and even corporations that are involved in recognition programs where certificates are in order. The market is large, diverse, and challenging—because there are many paper companies that offer computer programs for producing certificates having the same look as a hand-produced one. Consider branching out and offering both hand-pro-duced and computer-generated calligraphy, and you'll stand a good chance of continu-ing this fine and delicate tradition.

Start-up:

Calligraphy pens and paper are all you need to start this business, although you will have to work hard to get the word out. Perhaps you could mail invitations to those who might need your service, inviting them in for a free consultation. Networking with bridal salons may also help build business. Charge at least $50 for your services, since they are specialized and time-consuming.

Bottom Line Advice:

The freedom and creative nature of this age-old art form is in demand by those who still place value on the handmade; but, with the ability to quickly generate calligraphic style on a computer, you may find the market challenging, at best. Also, being a pro-fessional calligrapher isn't necessarily going to make you rich—but it's not a bad way to earn some extra pocket money, either.

Candle Maker

Start-up cost:	$150-$500
Potential earnings:	$5,000-$10,000
Typical fees:	$2-$20 or more (depending on size and intricacy) per candle
Advertising:	Local craft shows, specialty retailers, festivals
Qualifications:	The ability to learn a skilled trade
Equipment needed:	Wax wicks, scented oils, molds, flowers, baking soda
Staff required:	No
Handicapped opportunity:	Yes
Hidden costs:	Fire prevention and storage coolers

Lowdown:

The great thing about candle making is anyone can do it and it's really inexpensive. You won't get rich, but you could earn a tidy little side income if you work the arts and craft shows throughout the year. Your investment is low because nearly all of the equipment you need can be picked up at your local craft store or at grocery stores. There are different types of candles: hand-dipped, beeswax, honeycomb, confectionery, molded, and decorative. Decide early on what you'd like to specialize in, and try to set yourself apart by coming up with your own unique style. If you want to make some serious money at this, try to market to a crafts distributor (if you can really set yourself apart enough from the others they represent). If you're wanting to add variety, you might want to network with other candle makers and form a cooperative (that way, you can all save money on booth rentals).

Start-up:

Investment is so low that the first dozen or so candles you sell will more than double your profit (you could invest $150 at first). Depending on the kind of volume you want to produce, you could gross $3,000 for part-time work.

Bottom Line Advice:

Minimal skill is involved, so you can produce large quantities very quickly. If you want to specialize, for example, in confectionery (making wax look like a dessert, such as ice cream) or decorative (adding dried flowers), the process will take just a little longer, but you will be able to sell the items for more. The only drawback about candle making is that wax is highly flammable. If you're going to do this inside, use caution and keep your insurance policy up to date.

Caning Specialist

Start-up cost:	$50-$150
Potential earnings:	$1,000-$2,000 per month
Typical fees:	$25-$75+ per chair
Advertising:	Country magazines, furniture manufacturers, local paper, craft publications
Qualifications:	Should be an apprentice first
Equipment needed:	Cane, splints, rush, razor blades, scissors, tack hammer/puller
Staff required:	No
Handicapped opportunity:	Yes
Hidden costs:	Mileage for deliveries

Lowdown:

Before venturing into this profession on your own, you should be an apprentice, since caning is a time-honored tradition. It takes patience and an eye for detail to reweave wicker that has worn with time, or to add wicker to a piece of furniture that didn't have it to begin with. It helps if you are dedicated to the task at hand, because if you're good at what you do, you'll get lots of referrals, since there are so few caning specialists around these days. Still, caning is a slow process. Once you get an order, allow for soaking (about one day), drying (about two days), and making the chairs (approximately four hours per chair). You might want to partner with a chair maker to make your business more profitable; the two of you can copromote each other and provide a constant flow of referrals both ways.

Start-up:

Cane is sold in hanks (1,000 feet)—enough to make four chairs. Plan to pay close to $10-$15 per hank, depending on where you buy it. Total cost for materials is so low that, if you market yourself well, you could make a decent living of around $15,000-$24,000 per year.

Bottom Line Advice:

This could be a high-risk venture if you haven't done your homework or let potential clients know about your services; expect to spend a great deal of time promoting yourself in the beginning. The best part is you are considered a crafter and artist for the beautiful work you weave. For this, you'll need to like working by yourself and have enormous amounts of patience.

Career Counselor

Start-up cost:	$10,000-$15,000
Potential earnings:	$30,000-$65,000
Typical fees:	$350 and up per session
Advertising:	Yellow Pages, classified ads, job fairs, human resource newsletters
Qualifications:	Many states require certification
Equipment needed:	Computer, assessment software programs, TV/VCR (for educational videos), cellular phone, answering service or pager
Staff required:	No
Handicapped opportunity:	Yes
Hidden costs:	Any type of counselor must keep an eye on the clock if he or she is billing by the hour. Remember that time is money; clients often need to be told when their time is up

Lowdown:

There are literally thousands of careers out there—and many people simply can't follow the road signs. As a career counselor, you can assist them first with personality assessment, then with matching your client's motivations and interests to a potential career. Next, map out a success plan for achieving that new job or business (yes, many people do discover through career counseling that they would really rather work for themselves). You can use formatted questionnaires or conduct personal interviews (or a combination of both) to arrive at some career-forming conclusions. But your counseling efforts don't have to stop there; you can also offer resume services, viewing of motivational videos, cassette tape rental, and a library of resource books. The best part is, your business is recession-proof and corporations often contract with career counselors during periods of downsizing. The difficult part is reaching those who may need your services but are currently unaware that these services even exist.

Start-up:

Your start-up costs primarily reflect your office furniture and assorted resource/testing materials ($10,000-$15,000 is about right if you don't already have a computer). But the going rate for career counseling services is $350+ (depending on whether you're in a metropolitan area). With at least one good corporate client and a few stragglers, you should be well on your way in your own career path!

Bottom Line Advice:

You will be working with many different types of people, but they do have one thing in common: they have no idea what direction to take their careers. This can be frustrating to them, and no doubt that will translate into work for you which is part information-giving, part hand-holding. If you're well-adjusted enough yourself to help others deal with a career catharsis, you'll probably gain a lot professionally and personally from this type of service.

Expert Advice

Ken Lizott
Career Counselor

On Money Issues

Many solo practitioners, such as career counselors or therapists, love working with people but are uncomfortable with the financial aspect of their profession. Of course they want to earn a living, but they usually feel that they are not in their chosen profession for the money. They may hate sending out invoices, and might leave them undone for months. They might be afraid to ask for a fee or to ask for a more substantial fee. In short, there are a lot of issues surrounding money, marketing, and selling that a small business person must work out in order to be successful.

On Advertising

Word-of-mouth is by far the best means of promoting your business. In a relationship-based business, advertising does not work. Even if you have the best-placed, most expensive ads, you may not get any response from them. However, having a more relationship-oriented approach to getting the word out about your business, such as a job fair, is usually a good bet.

In our first year, we attended a job fair that included 400 employers with booths. My coworkers and I were the only career counselors there. For two days, 10,000 people came through the job fair, and perhaps half of them came to our booth. Some of those became clients, and others who didn't still spread the word about our operation.

Types of Business Insurance

- **Property Damage:** Covers fire, storm damage, vandalism, etc., for the replacement costs of the contents of your business.
- **General Liability:** Provides protection from personal injury and property damage.
- **Product Liability:** Protects from claims for damages or injuries related to defects in the products you make or sell. Regardless of outcome, litigation in these cases is time-consuming and expensive. Judgments often run to multimillion-dollar sums.
- **Disability:** Provides income replacement should you miss work through injury or illness. This is important if you are the major income source for your family.
- **Workers' Compensation:** Covers employees for loss of income and for medical costs arising from a job-related injury or illness. This coverage is required by law in all fifty states. You are legally required to: 1. provide a safe workplace, 2. hire competent employees, 3. provide safe tools, and 4. warn employees of existing dangers. Check the coverage of any contractor you hire.
- **Business Interruption:** Covers extra expenses and loss of income caused by an interruption of normal business due to an unforeseen event, such as fire. Lost income is defined as the difference between normal income and the income earned during the interruption of normal business.
- **Key Person:** Protects your business in case of the death or disability of an owner, partner, or key employee.
- **Health or Medical:** Protects against the costs of major medical expenses.
- **Special Insurances:** Many special types of insurance are available, such as automobile, crime, computer, life, malpractice, and glass insurance. Take a close look at your business to see what may be advisable.
- **Financial Insurances:** Depending on the structure of your business, you may need Sole Proprietor Insurance, Partnership Insurance, or Shareholder Insurance. Fidelity Bonds protect against loss from embezzlement.

Caterer

Start-up cost:	$15,000-$23,000
Potential earnings:	$30,000-$80,000
Typical fees:	$800-$15,000 per event
Advertising:	Brochures, press kits, direct mail, networking
Qualifications:	Cooking and menu planning experience, knowledge about sanitation and safe food handling, good people skills
Equipment needed:	Cooking equipment and supplies
Staff required:	Not initially; may be needed to grow
Handicapped opportunity:	No
Hidden costs:	In many states it is illegal to sell food prepared in a home kitchen; a commercial kitchen (which can be rented and/or shared) may be required

Lowdown:

If you have the right mixture of cooking know-how, business and good communication skills, catering can be a profitable and enjoyable enterprise. Though a commercial kitchen may be required, most catering services begin at home because start-up does not require years of training, expensive equipment, or capital investment. One fast-growing segment of this business is food delivery—especially lunches—to offices and corporations. Catering opportunities also abound in preparing private banquets at hotels, furnishing meals to airlines, cooking for parties, fund-raisers, and other events, or serving as an executive chef in a company dining room. Specializing in a particular item, such as gourmet wedding cakes or chocolate chip cookies, is another option. Caterers must observe health, safety, zoning, product liability, and other laws and regulations. Detailed record-keeping is also needed.

Start-up:

Access to a commercial kitchen can range from about $8,000-$12,000; appropriate equipment (pots, pans, etc.) will be $500-$1,000. In addition, allow $3,000-$10,000 for insurance, legal and insurance fees, license, and advertising. You will also need a delivery vehicle. You will have to lay out the costs of your "raw materials," but you can charge them back to the customers.

Bottom Line Advice:

Successful catering requires a lot of hard work and careful planning. You have to devote time to meeting with—and cooking for—potential clients even though you may not be chosen to cater their event. Social catering involves weekend and evening work, and is also often seasonal in nature. Keep in mind you also will be responsible for serving and cleanup, as well as menu planning and cooking, unless you hire others to do these tasks. On the other hand, cooking is fun! It's a creative process, one that nourishes the cook as well as those who eat the food. You can control how much or how little you work. And you'll always be welcome in everyone's kitchen!

Lease vs. Buy Decisions

If your start-up venture requires a lot of equipment purchases, you would do well to look into a "lease-option to buy" program that allows you to pay as you go. Why is this scenario more desirable than an outright purchase? Two reasons.

First, a lease allows you the flexibility of using equipment without long-term commitment to it. If, for some reason, your business goes under, you can usually negotiate your way out of a lease—and you're not faced with the prospect of having to find a buyer for your used equipment.

Second, your cash flow isn't tied up in equipment expenses—freeing you up to invest your capital in other, more immediate return areas (such as advertising).

Most leases run thirty-six to sixty months, but you can often negotiate your terms in addition to your rates. Since leasing is a very competitive field, your chances of finding a deal that is suitable to your needs are quite high.

Child Care Referral Service

Start-up cost:	$500
Potential earnings:	$10,000-$35,000
Typical fees:	$25 per client
Advertising:	Classified ads, bulletin boards
Qualifications:	Should be good at handling multiple tasks and somewhat detail-oriented
Equipment needed:	Answering machine, pager, or cellular phone
Staff required:	No
Handicapped opportunity:	Yes
Hidden costs:	None

Lowdown:

This is a perfect match for those who like to work alone and as a valued resource person. As a child care referral agent, you would provide names and phone numbers of reputable child care professionals in your area—at a cost of about $25 per caller. You would most likely get your start by placing a classified ad in your local newspaper, then scheduling a meeting time with the prospective client to discuss their needs and particulars with regard to the type of professional they're seeking. For instance, some career couples are in need of a caregiver to watch their kids all week long, while others just need part-time care for their children. Some will want individual care, others will want you to check out the local service.

Start-up:

With a $500 minimal start-up covering mostly your advertising and telephone costs, you could begin to pull in a profit almost immediately. You will need to build a vast network of child care professionals, which you can easily accomplish by posting flyers in public places (such as laundromats and grocery stores) and combing the ads in your local newspaper to find baby-sitters who are offering their services. If you have a little bit of extra money to play with at the beginning, you should also invest in professional-looking stationery and business cards to convey the best possible image to your baby-sitters as well as your clients.

Bottom Line Advice:

What's not to like about setting your own hours and having essentially complete control over a low-overhead business? The only obstacle would be limitations with respect to the availability of child care providers or those in need of them. If you live in a small, rural area, this business could max out in a month—but if you are in suburbia, you could really make some decent cash.

Childbirth Instructor

Start-up cost:	$500-$1,000
Potential earnings:	$15,000-$35,000
Typical fees:	$175 per couple
Advertising:	Bulletin boards, parents' newsletters, OB/GYN offices
Qualifications:	A nursing degree would be helpful—and respected by those needing your service
Equipment needed:	No
Staff required:	No
Handicapped opportunity:	Yes
Hidden costs:	None very serious (but you may want to invest in some educational materials such as models, books, and videos)

Lowdown:

Giving birth is a very natural experience that doesn't come naturally—that's why we need childbirth instructors to show us the way. First-time parents are especially uneasy (even frightened) about the pending event, and their fears are best calmed with detailed and expert information from a reliable source. If you've been in a delivery room, and have a nursing degree or related training, you would be a terrific candidate for this type of work. A childbirth instructor is essentially a teacher, so you must develop (and stick to) a teaching plan much the same as any other teacher. Most childbirth classes meet once a week for 4 to 6 weeks, so space your materials out accordingly. Begin with the basics and end with a strong visual, such as a childbirth film. Be sure to answer all questions, even the most common ones, courteously and compassionately—after all, many of your customers haven't a clue what they're in for, and it's your job to make their fears subside for a calm, secure birthing experience.

Start-up:

You will be competing against hospitals (unless you contract with them), so you will need to spend some advertising dollars to get your name out there. In addition to advertising in parents' newsletters, you might also want to consider advertising at a children's consignment store—they often have bulletin boards for related services and you could provide some referrals for them in return. Speaking of referrals, you should also get to know a few obstetricians and midwives; they will comprise your strongest source of word-of-mouth business.

Bottom Line Advice:

The birth experience is a joyous occasion, and you will likely enjoy telling and retelling the story of this miracle of life. On the downside, the repetition can get on your nerves . . . after all, how many different ways can you tell people how babies are born?

Clip Art Service

Start-up cost:	$3,000-$5,000
Potential earnings:	$15,000-$35,000
Typical fees:	$10-$15 per image or, preferably, a monthly clip service where you provide new images each month for a fee of $30-$40 per month
Advertising:	Business publications, direct mail to advertising/public relations firms
Qualifications:	A graphics or art background will help build credibility
Equipment needed:	Computer with high-resolution laser printer and scanner
Staff required:	No
Handicapped opportunity:	Yes
Hidden costs:	Your resource materials will run high at first if you use other people's clip art; if designing your own, watch for best prices on art materials

Lowdown:

Downsizing has severely affected the art departments of many corporations, with many now outsourcing to freelancers or buying predesigned work to paste into their presentations. Smaller agencies are also turning to nontraditional solutions for quick, inexpensive art. What is quicker and easier than copyright-free pictures that can be copied and pasted (or even scanned) into any of your business publications in a matter of minutes? The fact is, there are thousands of decent illustrations out there, whether in clip art books (available in most book stores for a nominal fee) or in software programs dedicated to specific themes (such as business art, sports art, cartoons, and religious art). The obvious problem with running a clip art business is that you're competing against literally hundreds of software programs that can do the same thing. Your major strategic selling point, then, becomes the fact that you have it all to choose from in one place, and that your availability is even better than overnight delivery. If you can sell your customers on those two concepts, you stand a fighting chance of making it. However, it would be wise to come up with an add-on service, such as cartooning or small-scale art production, to help you keep a steady income rolling in. Also, think of producing your own clip art and selling clients on the fact that it was specially designed by you.

Start-up:

Your start-up fees could be quite high, especially compared to your first-year potential earnings. You'll need to invest in just about every clip art book and software program you can get your hands on in order to build a sufficient enough library for clients to choose from, and that could cost anywhere from $1,000-$1,500 total. Next, you'll need to advertise in business publications or through direct mail to advertising and public relations companies, and that could run as high as $3,000. When you consider that your charges may be as little as $10 per image, it doesn't take a wizard to see that the return on investment will take a while. Your best bet is to try to design your own clip art and market it on a subscription basis to local companies; for a monthly fee of $20-$40, you could earn more money on a more regular basis.

Bottom Line Advice:

You'll really need to network with advertising and promotion specialists to get this business off the ground. Understand that people buy people, not just art, and that your biggest asset is personalized service. You can save companies time by searching through a myriad of resources for that perfect image—stress that point in everything you do.

How to Stay Positive

Let's face it, the best thing about owning your own business is that it is your own business. But, it has also been said that the worst thing about owning your own business is that it is your own business. When things are going great, it's easy to be positive, but what can you do when you have some slow times?

- **Take inventory of all the good things that have happened in the last month.** Write them down, and really appreciate them.
- **Put a "plus" sign over your desk.** At eye level, so you remember to try and remain positive at all times (especially when on the phone with customers).
- **Concentrate on the opportunities you still have.** So often, we expend all of our energy on negative things that happen. Focusing on the future will keep you from ignoring potentially great opportunities that you might have missed while wallowing in your sorrow.
- **Surround yourself with positive people.** If you've got friends in business, try to support one another in times of despair. Offer positive advice and encouragement—but, most of all, learn to accept it when it's given to you.
- **See, then be.** Picture yourself succeeding again, and your chances of success will nearly double. Never underestimate the power of creative visualization.
- **Don't give up.** Even the most successful entrepreneurs have experienced setbacks, so you're not the only one. Have the courage to go on.

Clipping Service

Start-up cost:	$1,500-$3,000
Potential earnings:	$15,000-$25,000
Typical fees:	$2-$4 per clip (or a monthly fee for a predetermined number of clips)
Advertising:	Local papers, business publications
Qualifications:	Be observant and read voraciously!
Equipment needed:	Access to a copier and various publications, word processor/typewriter, envelopes
Staff required:	No
Handicapped opportunity:	Yes
Hidden costs:	Subscriptions could run high as a whole; try to negotiate the best possible rates or use on-line services; postage

Lowdown:

Have you always clipped articles and pinned them to your bulletin board for future use? Or are you an avid reader who's always clipping and mailing articles to people you know? You just might be able to make a living with this rather obsessive behavior. A clipping service finds and copies articles of interest to various businesses, including pieces on the company itself and/or its products, employees, the industry of the business, competitors, and related subjects of interest. Being familiar with the local library system is vital, but even more critical is the ability to search using the proper keywords (in the Information Age, you can accomplish such searches fairly easily on the computer). Good research skills and use of a periodical index will save a lot of time and hassle. Patience and curiosity are richly rewarded for folks in this field.

Start-up:

A moderately powerful computer, a pair of scissors, access to a copy machine, and a little extra time and money are all you need to get started in this business. None except the computer costs very much (about $2,000), so you shouldn't have much getting in the way of an easy start-up. The service that is really being paid for is the time spent searching through literally hundreds of publications. Being paid by the hour rather than by the piece is best; there's no reliable way to know just how much press each company is generating without putting in a considerable amount of time. Get started by calling the public relations offices of local corporations to find out if they need this service; network in their professional organizations to drum up initial business.

Bottom Line Advice:

The most positive aspect of this business is its versatility. If you don't have a computer, finding a local library with convenient hours is likely the most difficult task involved. Using your own subscriptions is not recommended, since it limits the number of copies available and is more expensive. Watch that on-line time (write down all possible keywords before connecting).

Collectibles/Memorabilia

Start-up cost:	$5,000-$15,000
Potential earnings:	$500-$20,000
Typical fees:	Varies on what you are selling and the going rate for it
Advertising:	Flea markets, swap meets, antique fairs, flyers, brochures
Qualifications:	Knowing how to spot money from junk
Equipment needed:	20-30 collectibles to start
Staff required:	No
Handicapped opportunity:	Yes
Hidden costs:	Table/space rental fees

Lowdown:

Everything old is new again! Remember the Morton Salt Girl or the Brady Bunch lunch boxes with radios in them? They are in popular demand right now and bringing in top dollars ($100 or more each). And so is anything retro: salt/pepper sets, board games, clothing, limited edition plates, Presidential items, cereal boxes, you name it—but that doesn't relieve you of the responsibility to heavily market your service. You can specialize in one era like the '50s and carry everything from that time period. Or, you can specialize in one item (like toasters through the century). Try to hit as many antique fairs, swap meets, and dealer conventions as possible; that's where you'll spend a little, but earn a lot.

Start-up:

You will need equipment to show off your stuff, so that will be the biggest expense (about $1,000). The next will be your advertising and marketing. When you go to shows plan on paying $15-$100+ to rent a table or space to showcase your merchandise. Earning potential will be initially slow—$500-$20,000—until you've gotten established.

Bottom Line Advice:

People are crazy for the past. In some ways, it represents a simpler time in their lives, and that's something many people are willing to pay for. Collecting has become a $6-billion-dollar a year business, so if you have a collection you're willing to part with, you could make some serious money. Collecting interests tend to run in 20-year cycles, so this has a long-term possibility if you have an eye for what is collectible and what will sell. The danger is getting so caught up in acquiring certain pieces that you aren't willing to part with them yourself. Beware—collecting is intoxicating to those who enjoy it!

College Application Consultant

Start-up cost:	$500-$1,000
Potential earnings:	$15,000-$30,000
Typical fees:	Extremely varied; some consultants charge as high as $1,000 for this service
Advertising:	School and local papers, direct mail, Yellow Pages
Qualifications:	Familiarity with various colleges and programs
Equipment needed:	Computer, variety of available databases, reference materials
Staff required:	No
Handicapped opportunity:	Yes
Hidden costs:	Long distance phone calls and on-line time

Lowdown:

Nowadays the hardest part of getting into a college is choosing the right one; it's a vital decision for a young person's future, with far-reaching implications. Now more than ever, a bachelor's degree is almost a requirement to secure a decent, well-paying job. And although some high schools do have respectable advising departments, many do not invest the time and money into this important aspect of continuing education that they could and should. That's where you come in. As an independent college application consultant your services are in high demand in a low-competition field. What more could a businessperson ask for? If you are amenable to long hours of research and documentation, this business could provide you with just the academic challenge you need. Your biggest hurdle is problem-solving for high school seniors and their families, dealing with emotional/sentimental issues (primarily of the parents), and helping anyone else interested in entering college who doesn't have access to the information they need. You would conduct a skills/needs assessment, match them to an appropriate choice of universities, assist the customer in obtaining and filling in financial aid and application forms properly (and mailing them on time). You will also relay necessary facts about: ACT/SATs, placement tests (such as math, English, and foreign languages), degrees, and extracurricular activities offered by the school that might be of interest to the student, program requirements, etc.

Start-up:

A computer is the largest expense at about $1,500, if you choose to buy one. It isn't a necessity but it will tremendously speed the search process. College catalogs show listings of offered courses and a description of each, as well as some information about application procedures, fees, deadlines, and requirements and other general facts about the school. Buying many of these, as well as a few specialized publications that rate universities or give little-known information about them, will cost several hundred dollars, but it's the basis for your business. Placing only small ads will help keep advertising costs down to $100 or so, but the price of calls to colleges may add up quickly, so remember to monitor your phone time. Charges for these tasks could be determined a number of ways: per task, per package of tasks, hourly, or however else seems reasonable for the area and best covers the particular request.

Bottom Line Advice:

Good listening skills and problem-solving ability are your biggest assets in this business. Customers are trusting you with a very important part of their lives: their futures. High self-motivation and research skills will also help keep you enthused and knowledgeable about colleges and what's new on campus. If you enjoy being the middleman, then college consulting is for you.

Customer Service Tips

Getting and keeping customers is the challenge for any new business. Are your customers being serviced as well as they should be?

Here is a checklist of questions you can ask yourself from time to time:

❑ Are customers being helped in a timely manner? Are phones being answered promptly and cordially?

❑ Do problems get resolved quickly and productively?

❑ Are your customers receiving regular information, discounts, and other special offers from your company?

❑ Is your customer database being updated and added to constantly?

❑ Are your delivery services top-notch?

❑ Are all requests for materials (brochures, catalogs, etc.) being handled quickly and as professionally as possible?

❑ Is it easy for customers to order your product or service, or do they have to punch a million numbers into a phone to do so?

❑ Have you noticed a significant increase in referral business (a primary indication of excellent customer service)?

Customer service is not a one-shot deal; your business can only grow if you constantly maintain relationships and treat every customer as if he or she is a customer for life.

College Internship Placement

Start-up cost:	$1,500-$3,000
Potential earnings:	$20,000-$50,000
Typical fees:	$75-$175 (paid by student/parents)
Advertising:	College newspapers, campus bulletin boards, direct mail to parents
Qualifications:	Background in placement services would be helpful
Equipment needed:	Computer with printer, fax/modem, e-mail address
Staff required:	No
Handicapped opportunity:	Yes
Hidden costs:	Insurance, on-line time

Lowdown:

It used to be that companies offering internships contacted colleges to find students for summer or short-term work. But, in the ever-competitive '90s, such companies are relying increasingly upon services such as yours to bring them talent in exchange for small pay and experience. It's challenging work to find a suitable internship for a student (and vice versa), and you'll have enough resources to choose from at your local library. There are plenty of books that detail such opportunities, and there should be plenty of postings for internships through on-line services or the Internet. You'd have to work pretty hard to exhaust all of the possibilities. You'd be wise to market to the parents of students, as they are typically the ones with the foresight to see the importance of an internship; they also are typically the ones with all the money!

Start-up:

You'll need to have at least $1,500 for your computer system and another $1,000 or so for advertising in your first six months. Charging customers $75-$175 (depending on the size of the university or college market you're serving) will likely lead you to an annual salary of $20,000-$50,000 per year.

Bottom Line Advice:

Your work will be different every day, and the challenges will present themselves on a regular basis, too. Often, you'll work with folks you simply can't seem to please, or who don't come across as highly motivated. Remember that part of your job is to sell the student on the importance of internships—what they can mean later on to a job-seeking student is immeasurable.

Color Consultant

Start-up cost:	$2,000-$4,000
Potential earnings:	$30,000-$50,000
Typical fees:	$35-$75 per hour analysis
Advertising:	Local newspapers, business publications, direct mail
Qualifications:	Possibly training through cosmetic firm, paint company, or similar business
Equipment needed:	Color swatches, color charts
Staff required:	No
Handicapped opportunity:	Yes
Hidden costs:	Travel expenses

Lowdown:

Have you ever wondered exactly how the major automobile manufacturers and appliance makers decide which colors to use on their products? Or where the world of fashion comes up with the latest hues? They use color consultants—experts who know the entire spectrum of the rainbow, including minute variations and redefining nuances that are invisible to the untrained eye. It is essential that a color consultant have a strong understanding of color dynamics (how color affects people) in addition to the natural ability to distinguish slight color variations. The former is a learned skill, while the latter is an inherent talent that must be present to ensure acceptance into training and success in the field. Once established in this business, your days will consist of working with anyone from cosmetic companies to corporate consultations to group workshops to appliance/furniture manufacturers to individual analyses. People will look to you for the trends of the future.

Start-up:

Training with a company that is heavily dependent upon color and color dynamics is the biggest initial expense involved in becoming a consultant. Most often, the program is a week of intensive instruction on color theory and analysis, marketing techniques, and applications; expect to spend at least $1,200 on classes/certification (if available in your area). Other costs are directly related to visual materials to use in consultations and demonstrations (anywhere from $25-$1,000). Consultations often last an hour, with the average fee being $50-$75, depending upon the industry and geographic area of the country.

Bottom Line Advice:

Working with people is always a challenge, but more so when it involves personal issues such as what's aesthetically pleasing and what's not (which can be quite subjective). Staying on top of what's new in the ever-changing fashion world can be an exciting challenge, so if you like the idea of making other people look good and making money while doing it, this could be the career for you.

Comedy Writer

Start-up cost:	$100-$1,500
Potential earnings:	$10,000-$30,000+
Typical fees:	$25-$1,000 per stand-up piece
Advertising:	Industry trade publications, word of mouth, comedy clubs
Qualifications:	Sense of humor, ability to write clearly and for audiences
Equipment needed:	Computer, laser printer, video camera/tape recorder, business card
Staff required:	No
Handicapped opportunity:	Yes
Hidden costs:	Travel, union dues

Lowdown:

Do you have a talent for making people laugh—at themselves, each other, and the world? If so, and if you have the writing ability to boot, you could make a living as a professional comedy writer. However, it is an extremely competitive field, and you'll need to be decidedly different (albeit unusual) to set yourself apart from the rest of the funny people. Your best bet for starting out is to write your own material and perform it at a local comedy club's open mike or amateur night. Or, you can write material and try peddling it to your local radio personalities—they often buy material for their morning shows. To be a successful comedy writer, you should be organized, concise, and dedicated. You also have to be confident that your material is funny and be persistent in shopping it around.

Start-up:

The sky's the limit on what you can make, but be prepared to shell out some savings for hotels, travel, postage for your scripts, and union dues to protect your material. Expect to spend between $100-$1,500; expect to earn $10,000-$30,000 or more (if you write for Jay Leno, you'll obviously be paid accordingly).

Bottom Line Advice:

Not everyone has the same funny bone. The trick will be to find someone—anyone— who likes your material well enough to pay for it. There are lots of long hours involved shopping the studios, agencies, and other writers during the day and the comedy clubs and stand-up comedians at night. Keep in mind that many stand-ups write their own material.

Commercial Plant-Watering Service

Start-up cost:	$800-$1,000
Potential earnings:	$30,000-$60,000
Typical fees:	$25-$50 per day; some work on monthly retainers of $500 and up
Advertising:	Referrals, Yellow Pages, affiliations with nursery businesses
Qualifications:	Knowledge of plants' requirements
Equipment needed:	Vehicle for traveling to client businesses
Staff required:	No
Handicapped opportunity:	No
Hidden costs:	None

Lowdown:

Interior plantings are more significant in some parts of the country than in others, but almost all large businesses maintain some kind of greenery to soften their offices. Once you show these organizations that you can care for their plants and make them stay healthy and attractive, you will have the opportunity to develop an ongoing business that brings you a steady income stream.

Start-up:

Costs are minimal. You will need a car or truck to drive from client to client, and perhaps should consider business cards that you could leave near the plants to generate more business. Most larger plant maintenance services charge a flat monthly rate of $500 or more; if you're smaller, however, this will likely be a part-time job, earning you between $25-$50 per day.

Bottom Line Advice:

This is definitely a business for plant lovers. If you enjoy making things grow, you'll find plant watering to be a rewarding enterprise. However, there isn't much change from day to day, although you are in and out of different environments as you go from customer to customer. This is not a business for people who thrive on excitement.

Community Calendar Service

Start-up cost:	$3,000-$5,000
Potential earnings:	$10,000-$25,000
Typical fees:	$150/year for each subscription
Advertising:	Business and trade periodicals, organization membership, networking, direct marketing
Qualifications:	Energy, a very high level of organization, an outgoing personality, good writing skills
Equipment needed:	Computer, office suite software with powerful database program, high-quality fax/modem, copier, printer, office furniture, business cards, letterhead, envelopes
Staff required:	No
Handicapped opportunity:	Yes
Hidden costs:	On-line time, attendance at functions, organization dues

Lowdown:

This business is among the newest emerging businesses. You'll create a master calendar of public events for your community, or an annual publication that is sent to your client list of hotels, motels, restaurants, and other high-traffic businesses. The excitement comes from the fax; each week you fax a reminder-and-update sheet to everyone on your list. As you become established, gathering the information will become easier, as planners, public relations people, and event sponsors will be sure to inform you about their dates and events. Why does this work? Many individuals and businesses need to know this information, and they appreciate the opportunity to have information to offer free of charge to their customers. Everyone from politicos to florists needs to have event dates at their fingertips, and your service will be faxing it to them weekly. In short, it is your business to make other businesses look "in the know."

Start-up:

You will need the equipment to gather and print the information, and above all, the fax capability to broadcast it weekly. This should cost you between $5,000-$10,000; but, by billing $150 per year for a company's subscription to your service, you could easily earn back your investment in two to three years.

Bottom Line Advice:

Keeping track of dates is hard—that's why all those meeting planners and impresarios are going to pay you to do it. You'll need to be the kind of person whom bigwigs like to talk to, both for info-gathering and sales of your service. Writing it all up in an accurate, amusing manner is important, because you're competing against a myriad of free arts and entertainment newspapers and similar publications. Creating a service like this means a super marketing effort until you get established.

Consumer Researcher

Start-up cost:	$2,500-$5,000
Potential earnings:	$25,000-$59,000
Typical fees:	$25 per hour
Advertising:	Business periodicals, trade journals, Yellow Pages, networking, referrals, business organizations
Qualifications:	Business background, experience in consumer research, proven track record, excellent writing and oral communications skills
Equipment needed:	Office furniture, computer, suite software, laser printer, modem, fax, cellular phone
Staff required:	Probably
Handicapped opportunity:	No
Hidden costs:	Preparation of materials, utility bills

Lowdown:

Your experience in communicating with consumers will allow you to provide essential information to your corporate clients. How is their product viewed in the marketplace? How do people feel about it? What would they like to buy to go with it? How were they treated as they bought it? Would the average consumer be interested in trying a certain type of new sports equipment or baby chair? What is the most appealing approach right now in window treatments? Thousands of questions like these are the grist for your mill, and you'll arrive at answers via phone, mail, or in-person surveys. You will need to market your own services to show that you can find the answers to the questions that affect your clients' businesses. Each successful project should lead to further work. Estimating costs, and price, accurately will be challenging. Managing the workflow will also require considerable skill. You'll be moving from the big picture to the details and back again constantly.

Start-up:

Keeping in communication, tracking data, and reporting information clearly are all essential. Your office needs to support these functions (for a start-up cost of about $2,500). You could earn around $25,000 after the first year.

Bottom Line Advice:

Writing an effective questionnaire, or interview script, is no easy task. Clarity, simplicity, and effectiveness are all vital. Gathering and interpreting the data are much more challenging than just talking to people about a topic. You'll be helping your clients decide what knowledge about their customers is important. Then you'll present the results of your research in a clear, concise form. Business will build slowly as organizations become more confident in your skills.

Cooking Class Instructor

Start-up cost:	$1,000-$5,000
Potential earnings:	$10,000-$20,000
Typical fees:	$20-$45 per class
Advertising:	Newspaper ads, brochures, flyers
Qualifications:	Cooking experience, teaching ability, some marketing skills
Equipment needed:	Cooking equipment and supplies, a place to teach (if not teaching at home)
Staff required:	None
Handicapped opportunity:	Yes
Hidden costs:	Possible need to rent a facility to teach the classes; must have adequate stove(s), generous counter space

Lowdown:

Gourmet cooking and dining are both very popular right now. There are many television shows featuring chefs and cooks whose creativity pleases the palate, and gourmet restaurants and cooking supply stores abound. If you have (or can learn) the basics of cooking and have an interest in teaching others to do the same, this might be the business for you. You might check out the possibility of teaching in a home economics room at your local high school. This business can also be conducted easily from your home.

Start-up:

Start-up costs can be minimal if you already have the cookware and utensils needed. In addition, factor in the purchase of a professional stove, if you don't have one, and the cost to rent a facility for the classes, if you don't want to teach at home. Teaching at home is only recommended if you have a large kitchen. The costs of your raw materials will need to be factored into your class fees.

Bottom Line Advice:

A cooking class business can be very rewarding. Everyone loves to eat, and learning to produce delightful meals will please your students. Marketing is probably the big hurdle for this type of business. You will need to advertise; you might be able to find related businesses to sponsor you or to spread the word about your classes. For instance, you could build a relationship with the owner of an upscale kitchen products company or offer your classes as "continuing education" through a high school's home economics department.

Coupon Distributor

Start-up cost:	$500-$1,500
Potential earnings:	$10,000-$35,000
Typical fees:	$3-$5 per drop site or a bulk rate for mailings (usually $300 per thousand)
Advertising:	Word of mouth, cover letter with resume
Qualifications:	Postage meters and knowledge of postal regulations; a clean driving record
Equipment needed:	Solid, dependable vehicle
Staff required:	No
Handicapped opportunity:	Yes
Hidden costs:	Insurance, mileage

Lowdown:

Coupon books are a quick, positive means of getting a company's message across to consumers; what better incentive to buy than a discounted price for doing so? Producers of coupon books often don't have the time or resources to distribute the books themselves, so they hire out services such as yours to make sure that potential buyers receive their "golden" opportunities. You'll either drive around your community distributing such books by hand, or you'll use direct mail to ensure delivery by a specific date. Because coupons are of a time-sensitive nature, you'll always need to stay on track—invest in a good time-management system (a personal organizer or even a simple planner) to make sure that you never miss a deadline. Familiarize yourself early on with postal regulations; post offices regularly hold classes that teach you all the ins and outs of mass mailing. Networking with printers, advertising agencies, and coupon book producers will bring you the most business (rather than advertising your services in a publication).

Start-up:

If you already have a dependable vehicle, you'll spend between $500-$1,500 getting this business off the ground. Mostly, you'll spend it on postage equipment and your own self-promotion. You'll charge about $300 per thousand, or $3-$5 per drop site if you're doing it via your own vehicle. You can expect your annual earnings to be between $10,000-$35,000 (depending on which method you choose to deliver the books).

Bottom Line Advice:

This is a good part-time profession, but it isn't exactly dependable, as many coupon book producers are disreputable or go out of business in a short period of time. Align yourself with the tried and true, and all will go smoothly. Otherwise, you might consider becoming a coupon book producer yourself.

Credit Card Merchant Broker

Start-up cost:	$1,000-$2,000
Potential earnings:	$30,000-$40,000
Typical fees:	Commission on accounts accepted by bank; often an application fee of $125 or more per client
Advertising:	Classified ads, magazines targeting business people, membership in local business groups
Qualifications:	None (except sales ability)
Equipment needed:	Basic office setup
Staff required:	No
Handicapped opportunity:	No
Hidden costs:	Telephone bills for long-distance sales; mileage and car phone expenses

Lowdown:

Credit cards aren't always as welcome as they seem. That is, not all merchants accept them, or accept all kinds. Merchants want to deal with credit cards linked with banks, or set up their own credit cards through a solid bank. You will advertise your representation of one or more banks for credit accounts. You will help the merchants fill out their account applications. When an account application is accepted, you will receive your commission. You'll need to keep developing new customers, but businesses are being created every day in almost all communities. Most of these new businesses are potential customers.

Start-up:

This is not an expensive type of business to enter, but you will have to pay for your initial ads before commission revenue can cover the next batch. Expect to spend $1,000-$2,000 to develop professional-looking materials and good working relationships with several banks.

Bottom Line Advice:

Keep careful track of which advertising venues are productive for you. In this way you will gradually learn what publications should receive your advertising dollars. The grapevine is valuable to anyone like you who needs to know about new businesses being established nearby, although advertising and direct mail marketing can be targeted at new enterprises nationwide. You'll need to travel to the customer's location for the application fill-out process; after that, you'll do occasional follow-up to make sure their in-store credit cards are actually bringing in more business.

Dance Instructor

Start-up cost:	$1,500-$3,000
Potential earnings:	$25,500-$35,000
Typical fees:	$15 per lesson
Advertising:	Yellow Pages, entertainment sections of local papers, brochures, dance-wear retailers
Qualifications:	Experience, a degree to teach at the college/conservatory level
Equipment needed:	Studio, dance equipment
Staff required:	No
Handicapped opportunity:	No
Hidden costs:	Insurance, advertising

Lowdown:

Fred and Ginger made it look so good that everyone wanted to try it—and that's pretty much how the Fred Astaire School of Dance got its start so long ago. If you are an excellent dancer/choreographer yourself, and don't mind being patient with younger folks who aren't as focused as you are yet on the art of dance, you could dance your way into a respectable living. Physical strength, endurance, coordination, and creativity will help your business take off—but not more than referrals. Many dance instructors have years of training themselves or are retired from the profession. Some instructors will specialize in one area of dance such as tap or ballet in order to keep a cohesive following; others offer special packages where students can learn several different dances over a period of six to eight weeks.

Start-up:

The cost includes the rental of studio space if you do not have a large room to hold classes in (start-up costs could be as little as $500). The other part of your expense will be advertising your services ($1,500-$3,000). Earnings, however, are pretty decent if you have a good reputation and get regular referrals. At some levels, a dance instructor could make $40,000+ and a private instructor $27,000.

Bottom Line Advice:

The long hours, especially evenings and weekends, may hinder some from pursuing this career. However, the grace, beauty, and strength of dancers are admired by many. Patience and the ability to critique without being hypercritical should come naturally if you want to be successful.

Expert Advice

Judith Fortin
Dance Instructor

On Knowing Yourself

Not everyone who is a good dancer is going to be a good teacher. It doesn't work that way. A lot of people think that if they can perform at a very high level, they can walk into a studio and be able to teach. Teaching is a gift, and the principles that you use to teach dance are the same that you use to teach algebra.

When I first started teaching, I was renting a shared space. A lot of dance schools start out in church halls or school buildings. They may have use of the space for three hours, and then somebody else will be in there for the next three hours. I didn't really like that. So when I found my present studio, I chose a place I love and that is close to my home. But if I had placed it in a more commercial location, I think I could have done even better.

Day Care Service

Start-up cost:	$3,000
Potential earnings:	$25,000-$40,000
Typical fees:	$40 per child per week or $50 per adult per week
Advertising:	Referral service, bulletin boards, classified ads
Qualifications:	Some states require a license and insurance
Equipment needed:	For children: cribs, toys, movies, and games; for adults: arts/crafts supplies and some form of entertainment
Staff required:	No (but many states impose a limit on the adult-to-child ratio; for example, in Ohio you may have no more than six children to one adult)
Handicapped opportunity:	No
Hidden costs:	Insurance

Lowdown:

The day care business has been growing in direct relation to the rising number of women choosing careers in addition to families—and never has it been more flexible. There is a need to care for both seniors and children—and a few innovative entre-preneurs have integrated both at their care centers, so that the two groups can enjoy and learn to appreciate one another. You can easily start a day care center in your home if you meet the necessary zoning requirements of your community. It works best if you have a large yard and extra room (perhaps a finished basement) so that there is plenty of room to play. You'll need to be clear in your rates/policies (especially about regular hours, vacations, and payment due dates), and be careful not to let the parents treat you like a baby-sitter who is at their beck and call. Be assertive about protecting your personal time with your own family.

Start-up:

Your main start-up cost will be getting the word out about your service. Classified advertising, bulletin boards, and mothers' groups are a good way to build word of mouth. Your larger expenses will likely come from updating your home to meet zon-ing regulations; your home may have to pass inspection before licensing. If you decide not to license or not to carry insurance, be sure to let the parents/families know, because you will be held liable in the event of a disaster if you don't. Along those lines, be sure to familiarize yourself with safety procedures in case of an emergency.

Bottom Line Advice:

If you love to be around little people or seniors, you'll enjoy the opportunity to do so daily. Also, if you have children of your own, you can be paid for watching them play with others—not a bad position to be in. On the downside, although you are respon-sible for the children you watch, you are not their parent—a fact the parents them-selves may constantly remind you of. Be sure to meet with the parents of children or the families of seniors on a regular basis to keep communications straight.

Desktop Publisher

Start-up cost:	$15,000-$25,000
Potential earnings:	$20,00-$100,000
Typical fees:	$500 (newsletter) to $20,000 (for a large-run book or magazine)
Advertising:	Direct solicitation, Yellow Pages, local publications, word of mouth, networking, advertising in writers' magazines
Qualifications:	Computer skills, knowledge of typefaces, design, and layout, writing and editing skills, communication skills
Equipment needed:	Computer with scanner, laser printer, and CD-ROM, publishing, word-processing, and drawing software, fax, office furniture, business card, letterhead, envelopes
Staff required:	No
Handicapped opportunity:	Yes
Hidden costs:	Marketing; keeping up with changes in software

Lowdown:

Desktop publishing (DTP) enables people who understand graphic design and typography to offer a range of services to clients. Skills with computer software will allow you to produce books, flyers, and almost every kind of printed material in between. Many small DTP businesses succeed by specializing; for example, they might create newsletters for a specific type of business. Others produce entire books or focus on annual reports. Most will provide only the camera-ready master and subcontract the larger printing jobs to a commercial printer. The DTP field includes many small and large businesses, but there is room for people who do excellent work, produce it on time, and focus on their clients' needs and expectations.

Start-up:

The computer equipment required can be very expensive, depending largely on the graphics capability you need. And you must have a work space that supports the complex nature of some DTP tasks. Figure marketing costs, too, of $1,000-$2,000 in the financial section of your business plan. Your income will be dependent upon how many clients you can win in a short period of time, so you'll need to advertise your services (unless your former employer has become a major client). Billing can be done hourly ($50-$75 per) or, more typically, on a per-job basis. Smaller jobs can net $50-$300; larger ones can bring in $5,000 or more.

Bottom Line Advice:

Although working on several different creative projects at one time can be interesting and challenging, the pressure can be unbelievable. In the days of instant information and 24-hour turnaround, everybody expects their work done today. That can be a problem when you have 10 or more clients you're juggling—try to express realistic deadlines with your clients to avoid all-nighters and stress-filled days, and be sure to schedule time for yourself to complete the work.

Expert Advice

What sets your business apart from others like it?

Tim DiScipio, President of Easton Media Group in Greenwich, Connecticut, says he has a unique niche in the electronic marketplace. "I've got valuable years of experience in this field; something others can't claim in an emerging industry. It's attractive to companies that want someone who's been in the industry for a while and knows their way around."

Things you couldn't do without:

Obviously, DiScipio couldn't do without a computer (he has two), but he also needs a high-speed modem, a two-line telephone, and a fax machine.

Marketing tips/advice:

"If you're going to thrive in this business, you really need to network and expand your contacts regularly. Everyone in this industry has a different, unique niche . . . align yourself with the real players who can help you expand to where you need to be. Stay within your own niche; don't try to be everything to everyone."

If you had to do it all over again . . .

"I would have relinquished the time-consuming business operations duties and focused on my areas of specialty. It would have simplified my problems and allowed me to remain focused."

Understanding Your Cash Budget

For those business owners who are "mathematically challenged," here is a quick breakdown of the items that should appear on your cash flow projection statements. Basically, you need to look at what's coming in and what's going out on a regular basis.

"In" column:

- Cash sales
- Accounts Receivables
- Funds from sales of assets or equipment
- Refunds (such as tax refunds)
- Collections (outstanding accounts)

"Out" column:

- Inventory/stock purchases
- Operating expenses
- Fixed expense payments
- Credit payments on long-term debt
- Tax payments (most often quarterly)
- Shareholder/stock payments

Taking a look at these items and how they change over a period of a year can provide you with a Profit and Loss statement that clearly shows you what your business is earning and spending.

You can use this information to build your following year's budget, by making educated assumptions based on what happened the previous year. For instance, if you had a bad winter quarter because your business is somewhat dependent on good weather, you'll know to build sales up in the fall to cover your winter operating budget and make sure the bills get paid.

Desktop Publisher: Community-Based Coupon Books

Start-up cost:	$1,000-$5,000
Potential earnings:	$15,000-$30,000
Typical fees:	Ad rates vary (but generally start at $300-$500 per ad); plus, you can sell the books to the public for an average cover price of $29.95
Advertising:	Yellow Pages, community newspapers, local radio
Qualifications:	Ability to relate to both businesses and the public, one-on-one
Equipment needed:	Computer, software, printer
Staff required:	Yes
Handicapped opportunity:	Yes
Hidden costs:	Phone and mileage for ad sales reps

Lowdown:

You'll be providing a useful service for both the businesses and the public. Businesses offer discounts to attract customers; you are aiding them in their marketing strategies by publicizing these discounts. You will sell advertising space in your coupon books, produce them with a printer, and then sell them to consumers through the mail. If you enjoy people and are good at presenting your "product," you will find that many customers in your community are receptive to receiving discounts from businesses they know and respect. The best part is, your revenue is collected from both sides (the advertiser and the buyer)—so you have a double stream of income.

Start-up:

It requires a lot of legwork to get a business like this started, but the end-product—an inexpensively printed booklet—is your major cost. Perhaps you can strike a deal with a local printer, offering a percentage of the take. Or, shell out the $1,000-$5,000 in your first six months of start-up—if you sell enough ads and begin to generate simultaneous interest from the public, you'll make enough to cover printing (and still have quite a bit left over).

Bottom Line Advice:

You're creating a business enterprise out of almost nothing as you develop and sell your coupon book. This is truly a business that depends on hard work. Many individuals find a deep sense of satisfaction in knowing that they have provided a useful community service while making a profit at the same time. However, gathering enough coupon commitments from businesses is difficult: selling has its discouraging days. This is an enterprise for people with a lot of determination and a great deal of free time to successfully promote the book to the public.

Gaining Credibility

Once you've opened your doors for business, how do you get the customers to learn your name and trust it as a reliable source in the community? Ultimately, the way to build credibility is to develop a strong business with a solid reputation for delivering what it promises the customer. But what can you do in the meantime (until you're a household name)? Here are some possibilities:

- Volunteer at local charitable foundations and corporate events. Simply being out there where other influential types are likely to be found (either as sponsors or as participants) will put you face-to-face with people who can help spread the word about your business. It's worth the donated hours on your part, and you'll get to widen your circle of acquaintances.

- Offer yourself as an expert on your topic of interest. Send regular press releases with tips for consumers to local and regional newspapers and magazines. Editors love such items and you stand a good chance of being interviewed the next time a story on your area of expertise rolls around. Be sure to keep in regular contact with the press, even if it's just a quick phone call to ask if they need any help with upcoming features.

- Give free speeches at local association dinners. Or lunches. Or breakfasts. Really, just about anywhere where potential clients gather to learn more about improving their professional (and possibly personal) lives. Association meetings work best because they are always in need of interesting new speakers—so are civic groups and universities.

- Create and mail a regular newsletter with useful tips. Giving some information for free can create positive awareness of your company and what it has to offer. People do tend to read newsletters, and even though they may not need your services today, such publications (if well done) will keep you in their minds tomorrow.

- Perform to your personal best. Ultimately, it's going to be a reputation based on fair pricing, high quality, and exceptional service that will gain you the credibility you need to bring in new business. Set high standards and work every day toward achieving them, and you will have your credibility sooner than most.

Direct Marketing/Sales

Start-up cost:	$1,000-$3,000
Potential earnings:	$20,000-$50,000
Typical fees:	Percentage basis
Advertising:	Word of mouth, direct mail, cold calling
Qualifications:	Energy, persistence, ability to manage time well
Equipment needed:	None
Staff required:	None at first
Handicapped opportunity:	No
Hidden costs:	Some organizations charge for catalogs and other sales materials, attendance at meetings, inventory replacement

Lowdown:

Many, many people try their hand at direct sales, yet only a few of them make it big. What is the difference? Consider your goals. Do you want to make a few bucks and sell a line of products you like to family, friends, and acquaintances? Is your main goal to make your own purchases at a discount? Or are you planning to put the effort and commitment into direct sales that you would into establishing any other type of small business? Many products are best sold person-to-person because they benefit from demonstration. Finding an excellent product line to work with is vital, and you should feel confident in the company as well. The rest is up to your selling skills and personal drive. Many direct sales-oriented companies encourage their salespeople to create networks, additional salespeople whose sales bring a percentage to the person who recruited them. This practice acts as an incentive to everyone in the sales force. It is the way to large earnings, if you can achieve it.

Start-up:

Costs to start are very low (around $1,000), but watch out for hidden charges and fees from the manufacturers. These should warn you off the companies that might exploit you. An income of $20,000 in the beginning is realistic.

Bottom Line Advice:

How many opportunities are left in this country in which your own hard work will define your success? Direct sales is one of them. Are you comfortable with cold-calling? Are you committed enough to keep yourself going with no one to answer to but yourself? Do you genuinely like people and enjoy helping them find products that will add something to their lives? Or, on the other hand, would you be satisfied with direct sales as an add-on to some other activity? Be sure you're clear on what you want, and what you will need to do to achieve it. If you have big ambitions, you'll need a very big commitment to achieve them in direct marketing and sales.

Dog Trainer

Start-up cost:	$1,000-$2,000
Potential earnings:	$35,000-$45,000
Typical fees:	$300 for a three-week session is fairly common
Advertising:	Flyers, direct mail, Yellow Pages, classifieds, referrals from vets, free clinics
Qualifications:	Experience with different breeds, track record of success, patience, and credibility
Equipment needed:	Space for pets to roam, be fed, etc., kennel area for sleeping
Staff required:	No
Handicapped opportunity:	No
Hidden costs:	Advertising, travel

Lowdown:

Working dogs need considerable training, depending on the jobs they have to perform. Drug-sniffing dogs, guard dogs, guide dogs, movie dogs, and herding dogs all have their specialized training systems. Often these dogs receive much of their training from their breeders or owners, although some trainers of working dogs have national reputations for their skill and effectiveness.

A much bigger market is training services for pets. Most pet owners wake up a bit late to the need for training (usually after half of the carpet has been eaten), but you can present your service as the solution to those nagging problems that make pet dogs so frustrating at times. Some trainers give classes for owner and dog together while others go to a pet's home and provide individual sessions. Network with veterinarians; they are usually the first to hear about animal problems.

Start-up:

Your main start-up cost is for whatever marketing and advertising approaches seem best for your community. Somewhere between $500-$1,000 would be an average amount to spend on launching this business. Remember, though, that you'll be charging as much as $300 per dog for a three-week session—that can add up to a tidy profit early in the game.

Bottom Line Advice:

This job is immensely enjoyable if you love dogs and can tolerate their owners (remember, you'll be training them, too). Gaining the trust of an animal is an essential part of any training process, but some trainers find that getting the human side of the equation to cooperate is even harder. Once the pets in your class begin to give up eating the curtains and jumping all over Grandma, however, you will seem like a genius. Then the class can proceed to the really hard stuff such as coming when called (the pet) and being patient (the owner). For most trainers this is not a route to wealth, but a decent living can be made if you keep up your marketing.

Doll Repair Service

Start-up cost:	$500-$1,000
Potential earnings:	$20,000-$40,000
Typical fees:	Depends on what needs to be replaced and whether the doll is an antique (could be $50-$300 or more)
Advertising:	Yellow Pages, antique shows, specialty shops, hobby magazines
Qualifications:	Enjoying the art of doll-making and repair; special knowledge of antique dolls
Equipment needed:	Spare parts, precision tools
Staff required:	No
Handicapped opportunity:	Yes
Hidden costs:	Liability insurance, shipping

Lowdown:

This is a thriving business. As dolls get older, they become more popular to collect—and if they're going to be worth anything later on, they need to be in the best possible shape to command the highest dollars. One early Barbie doll can be worth as much as $500, but only if she's in mint condition. That's where you come in: you repair and restore dolls to their original state—and sometimes that means purchasing used dolls for spare parts. Keep all types of doll parts on hand and network with other repair services to locate spare parts. Pay attention to detail and have the hands of a surgeon. Dolls aren't just plastic—there are many different types, such as bisque, china, wax, and mechanical. Know what is special about each doll and what precautions to take when repairing them. Market your service especially hard at antique fairs and specialty shops. Have them keep your business cards by their cash register. You may want to offer related services such as collectibles connections (matching buyers and sellers) and a retail doll shop as well.

Start-up:

Advertising will be key to generating most of your business (about $1,000); the rest of your cost will go to spare parts (about $500 to start). Some may be expensive, so you may want to hold off ordering until there is a need. You will be repairing high-end and antique dolls, so gauge your earnings between $20,000-$40,000.

Bottom Line Advice:

Some doll repair services have given the business a bad name. You'll have to overcome this by knowing the ins and outs of doll-making. It is much easier to repair something if you know how it is put together. Take your time and know what you are doing; if you ruin a doll you may have to buy it. Be sure your packaging is secure when you deliver or ship to avoid any damage.

Doula/Midwife

Start-up cost:	$10,000
Potential earnings:	$20,000-$35,000
Advertising:	Parenting newsletters, doctors' offices, word of mouth
Typical fees:	$300-$500 per client
Qualifications:	Certification required
Equipment needed:	Dependable car, pager, cellular phone or answering service
Staff required:	No
Handicapped opportunity:	No
Hidden costs:	Liability insurance can be a killer; make sure you have good coverage

Lowdown:

If you appreciate the joy of bringing a new life into the world, this could be an ideal match. A *doula* (Greek for "woman's helper") or midwife takes part in the great circle of life on virtually a daily basis. After receiving your certification, you'll need to meet with family physicians to let them know about your services. Not all doctors will react favorably; however, women are demanding such services and look to their doctors for support. The rise in popularity of home births and homelike birthing centers in hospitals is another trend that could easily contribute to your success. One thing is certain: in this field, your best advertising will come from word of mouth.

Start-up:

Your training and certification costs (average: $10,000) will make for a moderate initial investment, but you should be able to recoup within a year after you start. You will, however, need to have liability and/or malpractice insurance, which can often run into thousands of dollars. On the patient side of your business, some insurance companies do not cover midwives—so you may have to work out payment plans (and collection methods) for these clients.

Bottom Line Advice:

The demands of being on-call for much of your career can take its toll—as can the occasional life-or-death emergency. Obviously, if you enjoy the challenges and aren't afraid of the risks, you can make a difference in the lives of a new family—and that may be your biggest reward.

See also: Lactation Consultant

Efficiency Expert

Start-up cost:	$5,000-$10,000
Potential earnings:	$35,000-$75,000+ (depending on your market)
Typical fees:	$75-$100 per hour or a monthly retainer of $3,000-$5,000
Advertising:	Trade publications, Yellow Pages, direct mail, business newspapers
Qualifications:	Ability to spot potential problems and time-wasters before and as they occur
Equipment needed:	Computer, fax/modem, printer, resource materials
Staff required:	No
Handicapped opportunity:	Yes
Hidden costs:	Insurance, underbilling for amount of time spent (watch your own clock)

Lowdown:

Corporations often have CEOs who want the company run like clockwork, particularly if there are production goals to be met regularly. As an efficiency expert, you will come into a company for a period of about two to four weeks and carefully monitor exactly how things are being done. You will ask workers questions such as, "Why are you repeatedly moving across the room to accomplish one simple task?" and "Is there any other way to minimize the steps involved in your particular process?" You are, in a sense, a detective searching for answers to the big question (which is, of course: "How can this company achieve more in a better and more economical way?"). Next, you'll print up a report or make a formal presentation, telling the CEO where he or she can improve operations. You should have a rather broad background in business operations, management experience, and a strong eye for detail. After all, your client companies will be paying you big bucks to figure out what needs to be improved upon at their facilities; you have to convey the idea that you're worth it, so watch your own image and always give it 110 percent.

Start-up:

Start-up will be relatively low (in the $5,000-$10,000 range), but you should do quite well when you consider what you might be able to earn if you're good at what you do ($35,000-$75,000 or more). You'll need a basic office setup and lots of good resource materials to help workers achieve greater effectiveness.

Bottom Line Advice:

While some corporate moguls will hire you to tell them what's wrong with their organization, they may not be willing to actually listen. You'll need to be clear from the beginning that you are merely offering your professional opinions and advice—that way, your personal liability will be kept in check.

Emergency Response Service

Start-up cost:	$1,000-$5,000
Potential earnings:	$15,000-$25,000
Typical fees:	$5-$10 per client per month
Advertising:	Yellow Pages, referrals from physicians/hospitals, direct mail, community newspapers, coupon books
Qualifications:	Superior organizational skills and the ability to respond quickly and professionally
Equipment needed:	Computer system with specialized software that recognizes alarms or signals, phone
Staff required:	Yes
Handicapped opportunity:	Yes
Hidden costs:	Insurance, system downtime (can be costly)

Lowdown:

Lots of elderly and handicapped folks have a limited number of caregivers, and many rely on the false hope that nothing bad will happen to them when they are alone. Your service provides peace of mind to both the homebound and their support people, because you are tied into their homes with a signal transmitter or push-button system that immediately contacts your computer. A signal goes off in your home, and you are in charge of sending immediate help to the client's location (which you've already got stored in your computer). It's fast, it's safe, and it's necessary for those who don't have much family around to call on them regularly. You will be in a noble profession, and there are some franchises you can buy into to get the benefit of technical support and even the specialized software program you'll need.

Start-up:

Your start-up costs will reflect a franchise fee (which, at $2,000-$5,000 is significantly lower than most buy-ins of a franchise operation). You will need to spend a little on advertising, but your computer system is what will cost you the most in the beginning (about $1,500). Some franchises include your computer as part of your buy-in. With or without a franchiser, you'll be charging between $10-$15 per client per month for your service; expect to earn $15,000-$25,000.

Bottom Line Advice:

Your clients will depend heavily on you for life-and-death situations; one time is all you'll get to make a serious mistake. You need to decide if you're in this to make money or to help people; ideally, it will be a mix of both.

Etiquette Adviser

Start-up cost:	Under $1,000
Potential earnings:	$20,000-$50,000
Typical fees:	$15-$35 per class
Advertising:	Newspapers, business publications, networking with community organizations
Qualifications:	Extremely good taste and a sense of moral superiority
Equipment needed:	Good resource materials
Staff required:	No
Handicapped opportunity:	Yes
Hidden costs:	Networking in high places could set you out some considerable cash in your entertainment budget—be careful not to live too well until you're making enough money to cover it

Lowdown:

You've always known the answer to seemingly eternal questions: which fork do I start with, and what is that spoon across the top of my plate really for? People rely on your expertise for such sticky situations as who to invite to a wedding, where to place divorced parents in a room together, when not to send a thank-you card, and how long is too long to respond to an RSVP. That's why your talents are needed, but how do you charge for them and still maintain your dignity? Easy—you offer your services in six simple courses. It's too difficult for an etiquette advisor to make serious money handling each question piecemeal, so develop a curriculum and offer your classes to the public or (better yet) the Corporate Confused seeking to become the Corporate Elite. You could offer tips on everything from proper conversation to handling potentially embarrassing situations; for instance, what should you do if your crouton shoots out from your plate to your bosses' during lunch?

Start-up:

Your start-up costs are so minimal, you needn't worry about whether it is proper to launch this business. Just make sure you have good reference materials for the questions that stump you—and leave a little extra for entertaining (which could be your main course to bringing in business).

Bottom Line Advice:

You'll love the authority and power of being a moral authority—but try not to let it get to your head. The last thing any one of your clients wants is a know-it-all. Be matter-of-fact, and try to inject some humor into your profession. Believe it or not, humor is the best teacher in a delicate, personal subject such as etiquette.

Fabric Coverings

Start-up costs:	$5,000-$10,000
Potential earnings:	$25,000-$50,000
Typical fees:	Varied according to project and square footage of area; can be as low as $150 or as high as several thousand dollars
Advertising:	Contacts with fabric stores and interior designers, news releases to home improvement editor of local newspaper, Yellow Pages
Qualifications:	Creativity and perhaps training in interior decorating
Equipment needed:	Heavy-duty sewing machine, shears, sample books galore
Staff required:	Not initially (maybe for larger installations)
Handicapped potential:	No
Hidden costs:	Insurance and unexpected fluctuations in materials costs

Lowdown:

Fabric is a creative alternative to wallpaper for the discerning customer to whom money is no object. The fact is, many Victorian homes used fabric as wall covering to provide a lush, almost ethereal appearance. You'll need special pastes and tools to smooth bumps and trim edges, and you'll need to have plenty of sample materials to show your clients to assist them in selecting the best choices. Network closely with interior designers and fabric store owners to gain some immediate business; consider waiving your fee for the first job or so (or until you get a good portfolio going). Offer a wide variety of styles and designs to choose from, and keep up with trends in the fabric industry by reading every publication you can get your hands on.

Start-up:

You'll spend $5,000-$10,000 in your first year of business, primarily to cover your training and materials. Sample books should be easy enough to come by (and many are offered by manufacturers free of charge). Your own fees will vary widely; they may be as low as $150 for a chair cover to $1,000 or more for wall covering.

Bottom Line Advice:

Careful, accurate measuring and treatment of fabric is necessary. Mistakes could be costly—and disastrous-looking, to say the least. Practice on your own walls first.

Fan Club Management

Start-up cost:	Minimal, if artist pays for expenses; $3,000-$5,000 if you're totally self-sufficient
Potential earnings:	$10,000-$30,000
Typical fees:	$10-$25 each for memberships; you can also derive a percentage from merchandising products
Advertising:	Direct mail and word of mouth
Qualifications:	Membership in the National Association of Fan Clubs
Equipment needed:	Computer, printer, fax/modem, copier, database/label and desktop publishing software, phone system with voice mail capabilities
Staff required:	Not initially
Handicapped opportunity:	Possibly
Hidden costs:	Postage and printing costs

Lowdown:

When a celebrity becomes a celebrity, the last thing they want to do is sit around answering fan mail. Still, many celebrities do realize that their fans are who put them where they are, and they don't necessarily want to ignore them. That's why it makes sense for popular artists to hire fan club managers to keep in touch with their many admirers: they recognize the importance of staying where they are by staying in touch with those whose opinions ultimately matter the most. If you have the right credentials (such as having been a professional writer or prior experience in radio or television), then you might be able to convince a celebrity to let you take charge of his or her mail. In addition to opening and answering huge bags of mail, you'll offer services such as quarterly or semiannual newsletter and merchandising (offering promotional products like T-shirts, posters, and autographed photos for sale and taking a small percentage for yourself). Like the celebrity, if you're in the right place at the right time, this could be the right opportunity for you.

Start-up:

You won't need very much at all to get started if you can convince a celebrity to foot the bill for his or her fan club; some celebrities actually do see the worth of paying someone else to handle the mail and requests for signed photos. However, most fan clubs operate on their own (with or without celebrity endorsement, but obviously it's easier with), leaving you with a start-up cost of $3,000-$5,000 if you operate on a shoestring. You could sell memberships for $10-$25 each, and offer incentives for joining (such as a free T-shirt or baseball cap). At any rate, you'll be producing newsletters (at $500-$1,000 each) a few times per year, so you'll need to be sure you've sold enough memberships to cover printing and postage rates. If all goes well, you could make $10,000-$30,000 per year doing something enjoyable and high-profile; not enough to make you rich, but certainly enough to make you smile.

Bottom Line Advice:

This seems on the surface to be a glamorous job, and it is—until you get barraged with unreasonable requests, tight deadlines on newsletters, and ego-maniacal celebrities who think treating "underlings" accordingly is the path to greater success. It might help if you continually remind the celebrity just how much more money the fan club is ultimately making them in boosting record or ticket sales.

Expert Advice

What sets your business apart from others like it?

"We are an authorized fan club management company and I have a highly specialized background in radio," says Joyce Logan, President of Fan Emporium, Inc., a Branford, Connecticut-based firm representing entertainers such as Michael Bolton, Carly Simon, John Mellencamp, and Mariah Carey. "I put myself in the fan's shoes and give every fan the personal touch . . . we produce newsletters, answer fan mail, sell authorized merchandise, and even have a 900-number service for fans to get concert updates and messages from their favorite superstars."

Things you couldn't do without:

Computer with a good database management program, printer and labeling program, fax, and modem.

Marketing tips/advice:

"Start with just one celebrity, and know that you can't just run a fan club for a little while. This is a serious commitment to the celebrity and the fans. You're dealing with people's emotional links to their favorite celebrity . . . you are a 'merchant of emotions.'"

If you had to do it all over again . . .

"I would have made contracts with the artists a little bit differently, so that they would assume all the costs of printing and mailing. We are a public relations firm just like any other, and we need to be recognized as such to stay profitable."

"Must-Have" Checklist
for New Businesses

Here are some of the more critical items you'll need for your new business:

❑ Computer system with a printer, fax/modem, and special software packages pertaining to your business and its needs (accounting, desktop publishing, etc.)

❑ Phone system with voice mail capability or answering machine

❑ File cabinets with a filing system

❑ Comfortable, ergonomically designed chair (often a last thought, but incredibly important to your productivity)

❑ Desk with plenty of arm space (for working on projects without bumping into your computer)

❑ Guest chairs and a conference table for meeting with employees, clients, and suppliers

❑ Bookshelf to hold your numerous resources

❑ Office supplies: stapler/staples, paper clips, pens/pencils, tape, corrective fluid, date stamp

❑ Storage shelves or cabinet (usually to store supplies)

❑ Garbage bins (don't forget one for recyclable paper)

❑ Background music (if that's important to you or your customers)

❑ Aesthetically appealing, yet professional-looking decor. Whether traditional or contemporary or eclectic, you need to send a solid visual message about your company through your decorative ability. If you are decoratively impaired, hire a professional to help (work out a trade for services).

❑ Most important: good lighting. One tiny desk lamp just won't do, and your staff will work as productively as you do if you invest in proper, clear lighting.

First Aid/CPR Instructor

Start-up cost:	$300-$500
Potential earnings:	$15,000-$20,000
Typical fees:	$10-$20 per participant
Advertising:	YMCA, hospitals, churches, associations, schools, swim clubs
Qualifications:	American Red Cross or American Heart Association certification required
Equipment needed:	"Annie-are-you-okay" dummy for practice (but you will be traveling to various sites to teach)
Staff required:	No
Handicapped opportunity:	Possibly
Hidden costs:	Some educational materials could cost you more than expected; you'll find out what you really need and what you don't from your training instructor

Lowdown:

The blond woman is stretched out on the floor, with a small crowd of people around her. "Annie, Annie—are you okay?" someone asks. She is not breathing, and one person gives mouth-to-mouth resuscitation while another provides heart massage to bring her back to life. Does this scene ring a bell? Many of us have been given CPR training at schools, churches, or swim clubs, and if you've always been interested in teaching people to save lives, this could be your calling. It is not particularly profitable (as volunteers from many associations offer similar courses), but you could set yourself apart by adding on a related service, such as a speakers bureau that offers tips on CPR in the Age of AIDS or some other topic of current concern.

Start-up:

It really doesn't cost much to instruct others on the benefits of life-saving techniques; your biggest up-front cost will be for the practice dummy and related resource materials such as models and diagrams. One innovative place you could offer your services is to restaurants; their staffs always have diagrams of what to do in an emergency, but do they really read them and have they actually practiced on anyone? Not likely. Offer them a group discount!

Bottom Line Advice:

The challenge of setting yourself apart from competing services offered free of charge can seem overwhelming at first—but get creative and you can make a small, yet profitable, business for yourself. Be positive and look for the big guys who can help provide a steady flow of business (e.g., health clubs, restaurant associations, and human resource managers at large corporations).

Flea Market Organizer

Start-up cost:	$1,000-$5,000
Potential earnings:	$25,000-$50,000
Typical fees:	$5-$100 from vendors per day, depending on size and reputation of market; from attendees, some flea markets charge an admission or parking fee of $3-$5 per carload
Advertising:	Flyers, classified ads, rent-a-sign
Qualifications:	Basic knowledge of the area and merchandise
Equipment needed:	Large piece of land (rented is better than owned), insurance, some form of shelter in case of rain
Home business potential:	No
Staff required:	Not at first
Handicapped potential:	Possibly
Hidden costs:	Liability insurance, crowd control, promotion

Lowdown:

Are you the type who simply cannot pass up a bargain? Do you consider yourself an authority on decent used or collectible items? If so, you might make a terrific "head flea." As a flea market promoter/organizer, you would round up as many vendors as you can safely fit into a designated area, and advertise everywhere your clientele would be likely to look for flea markets. The main jobs of the organizer are to promote the event to salespeople and customers alike and schedule the flea market so that there are no large competitors running theirs nearby at the same time. Another opportunity for the promoter is in selling goods to the public, and even to other dealers who've run short; you could make basically as much money as you have the energy to generate.

Start-up:

Two large expenses are the land rental and insurance coverage, each approximately $300-$500 depending upon the area. Advertising is key, but not very expensive (average quarterly budgets are $500-$1,000). Creating and making copies of a flyer is a good way to get the word out, as well as posting signs on local bulletin boards and en route to the site itself. Buying a supply of goods to sell is not necessary, but could increase profit by as much as 40 percent. Finally, two or more police officers acting as crowd control/problem prevention should be hired for at least $15 per hour. Charge anywhere from $5-$100 per table for vendors who wish to rent space; some flea markets also tack on an admission or parking fee for attendees ($3-$5 per carload is typical).

Bottom Line Advice:

The number-one priority in considering this business is organizational skills. A well-run flea market can make a great deal of money. Conversely, a poorly run event can be a disaster financially and logistically. (P.S. Make sure all of your vendors have valid vendors' licenses, or you could be fined considerably.)

Home Alone:

How to Feel "Connected" When You're Home-Based
You work anywhere from thirty to sixty hours per week in your cozy little home office, where you curl up with a cup of coffee and enjoy the solitude of working alone. No office politics, no petty disagreements, no feeling of corporate pressure.

But too much solitude can be a bad thing. When the sound of silence gets to you, where can you go for some human interaction? Here are a few places you can start:

- A home-based business forum available through on-line services such as America Online and CompuServe
- A professional organization made up of business professionals like yourself (check with your Chamber of Commerce for listings of such groups)
- Toastmasters International—this organization offers you the chance to improve your speaking/presentation skills as well as meet with several others in your community (and from all walks of life)
- Volunteer at your local hospital, community organization, or even professional associations
- Work one day per week at your local library
- Take yourself out to lunch; you can bring along an assignment and make it a "working lunch"
- Spend at least one-half day per week networking at a function or event
- Form a "business buddy" system with another home-based worker, sharing trials and tribulations
- Form a success team with a dozen or so other home-based business professionals, where you meet once a week to discuss your business problems and offer one another some solutions
- Stop feeling alone—there are literally millions of self-employed, home-based workers in the U.S. today.

Food Delivery Service

Start-up cost:	$1,000 or more
Potential earnings:	$25,000 and up
Typical fees:	$5-$10 per "run"
Advertising:	Brochures in office buildings, newspaper ads
Qualifications:	Ability to create attractive, healthy, portable meals
Equipment needed:	Kitchen, cooking supplies and equipment, food packaging
Staff required:	Part-time delivery person, if needed
Handicapped opportunity:	Yes
Hidden costs:	May need delivery vehicle; check out legal and health requirements

Lowdown:

Food delivery to the home or office is an idea whose time has come. Delivering lunches to office workers is especially lucrative. Harried people will love seeing your delicious dinner brought to their door as they arrive home after a long day at work. The menus need not be extensive, which simplifies the operation. You can "pick up" from a variety of local restaurants, or prepare your own meals. Challenges include safe food handling practices "on the road," keeping foods hot or cold, as appropriate, and maintaining on-time deliveries.

Start-up:

This business isn't costly to start up, especially if you opt to offer a lunch-only service. If you offer sandwiches and soups, salads and rolls, beverages and dessert, for instance, you need very little equipment to prepare the meals. You will need to invest in packaging for the foods (disposable plastic bowls, cellophane or foil wrapping, for instance); the cost will vary depending on the foods you're selling. Create a flyer that can be posted in heavily populated office complexes to get started; always deliver the next day's menu with each meal as you drop them off. Make sure your insurance policy will cover your vehicle while it is being used for deliveries and, if you are hiring a delivery helper, make sure your insurance covers that employee in your car.

Bottom Line Advice:

Most people in the food delivery business get up early in the morning to bake and/or cook; night owls may not survive! Expect a long day of work, especially if you deliver at dinnertime in the evening. You'll need an ability to deal successfully with vendors and suppliers to keep your costs down and the food quality consistent. On the upside, the future is bright for food delivery businesses. More and more people have less and less time to cook; everyone is tired of the typical "fast food." Start-up costs in most cases are modest, and you can net $70-$100 a day right from the start (the sky is the limit after that, as you add more routes).

Freelance
Writer/Editor/Illustrator

Start-up cost:	$2,000-$5,000
Potential earnings:	$22,500-$50,000
Typical fees:	$50-$150 per hour, depending on area and experience level
Advertising:	Personal contacts, trade publications
Qualifications:	Writing and communication skills; attention to detail and organizational ability, sense for graphics and design
Equipment needed:	High-end computer with light pen or graphics tablet and a high resolution graphics video card, scanner, laser printer, word processing, design, and contact management software, fax, office furniture, reference books, business cards
Staff required:	No
Handicapped opportunity:	Yes
Hidden costs:	Maintaining personal contacts (business lunches, etc.), memberships in trade organizations, software upgrades

Lowdown:

Many people have made careers out of freelance writing, editing, and illustrating—and many more are trying. Success will come for you when you can distinguish your services from those of others who will work for peanuts. Excellent communication skills are required to discover exactly what your clients want and need. You then turn those skills around to produce the corrected materials, written texts, or illustrations that will support your clients' marketing plans. This is a personal business that requires building up trust slowly and carefully before you can obtain the big projects that bring in enough income to make you successful. Creativity and goal-directedness are both essential. No detail can slip by your eye. But successful projects will bring you referrals, and each small step can lead to a bigger one.

As a writer, you will work on special editorial projects for clients ranging from small business owners to universities to newspapers—and you may even be lucky enough to snag a corporate client or two in the meantime. Your projects might be as specialized as an article for a trade journal or a corporate history; then again, you could be a generalist who writes articles on a wide variety of topics for various magazines and newspapers. Your best bet, at least in the beginning, is to produce brochures for small businesses.

As an editor, you will focus your energies on making sure everything that you see goes back out to a publisher totally free of mistakes—including grammatical errors, spelling and punctuation mistakes, and even poor sentence flow. Your job is to ensure that all the words on the page make sense and have a certain rhythm to them, so that the reader is carried along through the book logically and concisely. You may end up editing thousands of projects, from annual reports to menus to book-length manuscripts.

As a freelance illustrator, you will market your work to various publishing houses, ultimately in search of a regular contract with at least one. If you do secure a contract, you may design and produce book covers as well as any artwork to go into the book itself. This area of expertise is particularly lucrative for those who can produce lively, entertaining illustrations for children's books. If you should decide to stay unaffiliated with a large publishing house, your projects will always be varied and you'll have the challenge of getting to know what each of your client companies wants—over and over again. Many illustrators adore that challenge.

Start-up:

You'll be spending a lot of time in your office, so whether you plan to meet clients there or not, you'll need to make it an effective work space. The high-end computer equipment needed to produce professional results is costly, averaging $2,000-$5,000. Your hourly rates should cover all of your overhead, so price yourself competitively in the $75-$150 per hour range.

Bottom Line Advice:

You can indulge your love of words and graphics to the max in this field. You will be learning something new with each project, and you will have the satisfaction of seeing everything you produce be published (unlike poets and novelists). Working to support your client businesses can result in a satisfying partnership. However, pricing your services can be very difficult. Nonwriters often do not appreciate the time and effort that goes into producing an effective piece of writing, and there are many writers out there in the marketplace who are likely to undercut you. You'll have to spend long hours staring at your blank computer monitor and then actually completing the projects you have fought so hard to get. Deadlines are always too short, and sometimes it can be difficult to obtain the background information needed from a client. Freelance writers have earned the circles under their eyes the hard way.

Expert Advice

What sets your business apart from others like it?

Ruth Dean, owner of The Writing Toolbox in Akron, Ohio, says her business is unique because she listens well and helps clients clarify their ideas and plans. She specializes in technical marketing communications and gets her best results by writing to appeal to the client's intended audience, not just to the client.

Things you couldn't do without:

"The fax is essential. Clients want instant communication." A computer and laser printer would also be necessities.

Marketing tips/advice:

Dean markets by networking. "I just ask clients about their business and listen. That's all it takes. It's important to have writing samples available in simple 'packages' so that clients who are not accustomed to working with writers can figure out how to hire you."

If you had to do it all over again . . .

"I wouldn't have waited so long to go out on my own."

Networking Tips

- The best time to make new contacts is when you don't need them. It's best to call on others in happy times so that your business image is positive, and new contacts will respect you before you need help.
- Don't forget to follow up. Most of all, never forget to say "thank you."
- Set up a good filing or business card management system. Choose one that will actually work for you, not one that merely sounds good.
- Weed out nonproductive relationships every six months. But don't throw away a card if you can help it. You never know when you'll need that person in the future.
- **MOST IMPORTANT, ALWAYS BE YOURSELF.** We all have different styles of networking, and there are no real hard-and-fast rules when it comes to the joy of meeting new people—and making new friends.

Fund-Raising Firm

Start-up cost:	$2,000-$5,000
Potential earnings:	$25,000-$35,000
Typical fees:	Some fund-raisers charge a flat fee (varied) while others are paid about 20 percent of the total funds they raise
Advertising:	Direct solicitation, networking, referrals
Qualifications:	People skills, selling ability, excellent writing ability
Equipment needed:	Computer, printer, office suite software, fax/modem, office furniture, business cards, letterhead, envelopes
Staff required:	No
Handicapped opportunity:	Yes
Hidden costs:	On-line time, telephone charges

Lowdown:

You need to able to make the general public see the worthiness of the causes for which you are raising funds. This process has similarities to marketing any intangible product. Fund-raisers know a lot about the organizations they support and they believe in the importance of their missions. The other side of the equation is friendliness. You need to be someone that people like, respect, and feel comfortable with. They are effectively taking your word about the charity you are working for, so your word needs to be very convincing. A range of public and private organizations survive on fund-raising, so once you can demonstrate success, you will have a large market for your services.

Start-up:

Equipping your office is the main expense here, and you can add elements over time, once your telephone is installed. If you don't already have a computer, expect to spend at least $2,000 on one. Your earnings will largely depend on what kinds of funds you're able to bring in—not an easy way to earn a living, but profitable for the most tenacious.

Bottom Line Advice:

Fund-raising is done by charities and service organizations of all types, and even government-funded groups need to supplement their annual budget with funds gathered from donations. If you can help bring in donations, you can take this business wherever you want it to go. Unfortunately, a lot of other people have had the same idea, and some of them have been so dishonest as to cast the whole profession in a very bad light. Separating yourself from the sleaze will be an ongoing task for you. Expect a lot of hang-ups from cold calls, too.

Juggling Family and Work

Let's face it, raising a family and growing a business are each full-time jobs. So, how can you give 100 percent to each and still maintain your sanity?

First of all, set aside a special time each day or week that is designated "family time." During this time, you will accept no phone calls, set no appointments, and not even think about your business. You will probably not even want to stay near your office. Think about going out to dinner and sharing the three best things that happened to each family member during that week.

Or, if you feel you can incorporate your family into parts of your business, it might help them to better understand your needs and constraints. It's one thing for your spouse or children to see you completely stressed out; it's quite another for them to be in your office when that high-volume order comes in on short notice. Especially for children, it is a good idea to demonstrate your commitment to your work.

Smaller children, particularly females, need positive workplace role models— and who better to pave the way than Mom or Dad? Historically, children who are raised by entrepreneurs do tend to become entrepreneurs themselves.

What should you do in the event that a client or customer wants to meet during one of your special family times? You can handle it one of two ways: first, you could rearrange your family time. But the better solution might be to simply say, "I am already meeting with a client at that time . . . is there another time that works for you?" Others will respect your attention to commitments, and you never have to offer an explanation for whom you're meeting with, and why.

However you decide to work your children into your business, or your business into your family life, one thing is for sure: there will never be a time without challenges and disruptions.

You will need to develop the skill to work around any obstacle or challenge, and the best way to accomplish a good balance between work and home life is to learn to follow a time-management program. Scheduling your time is the best way to make sure everything gets done. The rest is just recognizing that it is possible to have two loves: your business and your family.

Garage Sale Coordinator

Start-up cost:	$500-$700
Potential earnings:	$15,000-$25,000
Typical fees:	Often a flat fee of $25-$50 per garage sale; sometimes an additional percentage (5 to 10 percent)
Advertising:	Classified ads, bulletin boards, community newspapers, condo associations
Qualifications:	Organizational skills, strong marketing ability
Equipment needed:	Phone, computer with letter-quality printer, fax, hammer and nails for posting signs
Staff required:	No
Handicapped opportunity:	Yes
Hidden costs:	Gas and mileage may get out of hand; try to cover these costs in your fee

Lowdown:

Are you a garage sale goddess? Do you spend your entire weekend cavorting around town in search of great bargains? This could be a business made in heaven expressly for you. As a garage sale coordinator/marketer, you would first advertise your services stressing your skill at saving folks time and energy so that they can relax and make money from their old stuff. Then you would organize all of the details involved in putting together a successful garage sale, including marketing (posting signs and placing publicity in newspapers, etc.), and running the sale itself (tagging, bartering, and keeping a record of what's been sold). Don't wait for the individual, single-home customers to build your business; try to work with condo associations, churches, and apartment complexes to organize large-group garage sales—these will bring in your best dollars and provide you with the greatest marketing opportunity, since many bargain hunters like the idea of one-stop shopping.

Start-up:

This business could be a real bargain for you, because it involves minimal start-up cost and the ability to be paid for something you truly enjoy. Advertising in the newspaper classifieds will be your biggest cost, averaging $500-$700. You can earn a pretty good penny for yourself in all of this, especially when you work with large groups. Charge between $25-$50 per individual garage sale, and add on a percentage of the profits if you'd like (5 to 10 percent is typical).

Bottom Line Advice:

Many large newspapers offer free garage sale kits, complete with signs, records, and tips for making a garage sale a success. Call or write to request one of these kits—they could become a standard for your business and make your job even easier.

Gardening Consultant

Start-up cost:	$5,000-$10,000 (more if you need to purchase a vehicle)
Potential earnings:	$40,000-$60,000
Typical fees:	Varied; can be as low as $125 or as high as several thousand dollars per project (depending on whether you're working for an individual or a corporation)
Advertising:	Yellow Pages, community newspapers, city magazines, direct mail, bulletin boards, networking, speaking to community organizations
Qualifications:	Extensive knowledge of plants, growing seasons, and regional climates
Equipment needed:	Gardening tools, hoses, seeds, perhaps a van
Staff required:	Yes (1-5 people to work on several projects simultaneously)
Handicapped opportunity:	Not likely
Hidden costs:	Liability insurance and workers' compensation

Lowdown:

There's nothing lovelier in the springtime than a perfectly planned garden in bloom. If you've always been the type who can effectively plan such perennial pleasures, you would likely be well-suited to this line of business. Especially if you don't mind working outside in the dirt for long periods of time during the warmest times of the year. As a gardening consultant, you will meet with either homeowners or business owners to work out the details of what will bloom where. Develop a portfolio of your best work, then reel in more business through speaking engagements or presentations to community organizations that are always looking for gardening experts because they appeal to large groups of people. Be sure to always be clear on what your services entail— many well-meaning folks will confuse your services with those of professional landscapers. If you don't cut grass, say so.

Start-up:

If you've already been involved in gardening, you likely have many of the tools you'll need to start. However, keep in mind that you'll probably be adding a staff once the phone starts ringing, so you'll need to double or possibly triple the number of tools you have on hand. Also, if you need a vehicle, such as a van, consider leasing and applying a magnetic sign to the door advertising your services. All said and done, you'll shell out about $5,000-$10,000—more if you add staff. But your fees, which will vary from $125 to several thousand dollars, should help offset any costs.

Bottom Line Advice:

Plan your speaking engagements and other forms of promotion during the off-season; chances are, you'll be too busy during the spring and summer months.

Genealogical Service (Family History Writer)

Start-up cost:	$500-$1,500 (depending on whether you have a computer)
Potential earnings:	$15,000-$25,000
Typical fees:	$25-$125 per search; $200-$500 per written family history
Advertising:	Magazines with a historic slant, newspapers, Yellow Pages
Qualifications:	None
Equipment needed:	Computer with family tree software program
Staff required:	No
Handicapped opportunity:	Yes
Hidden costs:	If you're billing on a per-job basis, don't spend too much time on each project

Lowdown:

Everyone would like to know their roots, and what better way to find out than through a genealogical service? By hiring such a service, you could learn about everyone from the first generation of your family to the black sheep that every family seems to have. As a family history writer, you would meet with family members to obtain every known detail about a family—and then compile the information into a family tree diagram or a written report. Mind you, not all is known about every member of every family, but the Mormon church has an extensive genealogical service that you could use to find seemingly obscure bits and pieces. And this service is provided for everyone, not just for Mormons. There are also census reports at major metropolitan libraries to assist you with your search. If you aren't afraid of a lot of research and detail-oriented writing work, this could be a great business for you. Every family has a different, yet fascinating, story to tell.

Start-up:

You'll need to have a good computer system and genealogical software to produce the kinds of detail-oriented reports necessary in the family history writing business. Expect to spend anywhere from $500-$1,500 on those items alone, then factor in your advertising costs at around another $350-$500 and up (depending on the size of the publication you advertise in).

Bottom Line Advice:

Your work is much in demand in these nostalgic times, and while there is not a high upfront investment, your time is worth money—and you could spend more of that than you are paid for. Make sure you budget your time accordingly or you could easily (and quickly) come up short.

Gerontology Consultant

Start-up cost:	$500
Potential earnings:	$25,000-$40,000
Typical fees:	$20-$40 per hour
Advertising:	Direct mail, networking with psychologists and medical professionals, speaking engagements
Qualifications:	Background in psychology or sociology
Equipment needed:	No
Staff required:	No
Handicapped opportunity:	Yes
Hidden costs:	None (but watch your mileage)

Lowdown:

Into the next century, the population over the age of 60 is expected to rise to as high as 65 percent of the total population. That's because many of us have chosen healthier lifestyles—but also because life expectancy itself is on the rise. With more and more folks still in control of their lives after age 80, the need for skilled professionals to help others understand the process and effects of aging will become more apparent. As a gerontology expert, you will work in conjunction with hospitals and psychologists to help patients and their families adjust to the many changes and challenges of their loved ones growing older. You will counsel them on issues ranging from health care to assisted living programs, and may be called on frequently as a resource person for hospitals and the community at large.

Start-up:

Assuming that you have the necessary credentials (i.e., a college education in psychology or a related field), your start-up costs should be minimal. The first thing you'll need is professional-looking stationery and business cards, so allow about $500 for that and some preliminary advertising. A gerontology consultant works primarily on-site; that is, at the place where your services have been contracted. Because of this, you can easily use your home as an office, but do make sure you have dependable transportation.

Bottom Line Advice:

You will probably enjoy the favorable attention you'll receive from people in need of your services, but you should also keep in mind that many of your clients are under unbelievable stress because they are balancing their careers with the need to care for aging relatives. They simply can't be in two places at once, and they may be difficult to deal with at times as a result.

Gift Basket Business

Start-up cost:	$5,000-$15,000
Potential earnings:	$25,000-$45,000
Typical fees:	Baskets are individually priced from $25-$350
Advertising:	Local newspapers, flyers, bulletin boards, direct mail to busy executives, Yellow Pages
Qualifications:	Natural creativity mixed with a strong business sense
Equipment needed:	Baskets and gift materials, glue gun, shrink wrap machine, delivery vehicle
Staff required:	No
Handicapped opportunity:	Yes
Hidden costs:	Shipping costs

Lowdown:

There's nothing nicer to receive than a basket full of goodies meant especially for you. That's why gift basket businesses have been cropping up everywhere. Some are even offered as franchise opportunities. On the surface, this business seems so simple anyone could do it: you just round up a bunch of neat items, place them in a basket, put ribbons and shrink wrap around all and voila! But there is much more to it than that; you must also be a gifted buyer (to get the best bargains on gift items and materials) and a real go-getter of a salesperson to bring in the constant flow of business needed to stay afloat. In other words, you should have all the marketing skills of a seasoned retailer in addition to a dynamic and creative mind. If you can handle all of that, you will likely succeed if your market area isn't already saturated. Be sure to set yourself apart from the others as much as possible: since there are so many in this emerging and trendy business, the competition is fierce and you'll lose out if you don't carve an interesting niche for yourself. Perhaps you could fill your gift baskets with only a particular type of product, such as products manufactured only in your state, or special theme packages.

Start-up:

Your start-up costs hinge on whether you're investing in a delivery vehicle or merely using your own car or van. You'll need to advertise heavily in places your customers are most likely to think of needing your services, and that will run you in the neighborhood of $500-$3,000. Your money will come from the gift baskets you sell (minus production and commission costs); most gift basket businesses offer a wide range of prices for an array of baskets, anywhere from $25-$300.

Bottom Line Advice:

Everyone is trying to get into this seemingly easy business. If you feel you can create a gift basket business that truly stands apart in some way, you stand a good chance of earning a living. If you're unsure about this critical piece of advice, rewrite your business plan. It's so competitive that you have to have a niche to survive unless you're in a remote part of the country (but, then, your customer base will also be limited). Still, if you're creative about gift baskets, you'll be creative in coming up with a way to sell them.

Graphologist

Start-up cost:	$500-$1,000
Potential earnings:	$10,000-$50,000
Typical fees:	$30-$50 per hour; if working with banks, often a monthly retainer of $1,000
Advertising:	Classified ads, business publications, banking publications/newsletters, networking
Qualifications:	Training in character details/nuances of handwriting; certification would lend greater credibility
Equipment needed:	A good eye, magnifier; some use computer and scanner to analyze handwriting on the computer
Staff required:	No
Handicapped opportunity:	Yes
Hidden costs:	Travel expenses

Lowdown:

With inventions like computerized scanning and computer programs that can mimic a person's handwriting, it doesn't take a genius to see that the job of the forgery expert has been made easier than ever. Important items such as checks, credit cards, and insurance policies can be processed by tellers and other professionals who are skilled in their work but not in detection of fake signatures. That's where the graphologist's, or handwriting expert's, special ability comes in. As a handwriting expert, you will work on a contractual basis with banking institutions and insurance companies, combing through suspect documents to look for the nuances that make each individual's written words different and distinct. You will identify and mark each curve of every letter in your search for similarity, and assist in prosecuting the guilty forgers once they are apprehended. You may even have to appear as an expert witness, and can sell your services to the criminal market in this manner as well. You would do well to work on a contract basis with banks and other institutions, but to offer yourself as an expert witness for hire as well. Expert witnesses can earn up to $500 per day for their time and opinions in criminal matters.

Start-up:

You may need certification in some states to work in federal institutions; if you do, set aside another $500 or so for courses and/or testing. Even with certification costs, your start-up will be minimal for this business. You'll need some business cards, stationery, and related office materials (about $500-$700); spend a little more than that ($300) on direct mail or advertising in a business publication. You'll charge at least $30-$50 per hour for your work, and you'll earn about $1,000 per month if on a retainer for a bank or other large business.

Bottom Line Advice:

If you aren't afraid of detailed work, graphology has a lot to offer.

Greeting Card Sender

Start-up cost:	$5,000-$10,000
Potential earnings:	$20,000-$30,000
Typical fees:	$2-$3 per card
Advertising:	Direct mail, Yellow Pages, networking, business publications
Qualifications:	Highly organized
Equipment needed:	Computer with database and labeling software, laser printer, fax, phone, greeting card sample books or brochures
Staff required:	No
Handicapped opportunity:	Yes
Hidden costs:	Postage can be tricky, as can untimely price increases from vendors

Lowdown:

Busy executives barely have the time to run personal errands of a critical nature, let alone send out 500 holiday greeting cards to their best customers. That's where you come in. As a professional greeting card sender, you will develop a database of card recipients for as many clients as you can muster—then mail the cards to everyone on the list. It sounds quite simple, really, and it is—except that you need to be exceptionally skilled at organization and time management to be able to stay on top of every holiday, birthday, special occasion, and company announcement that comes along. Buy a software program that features a large calendar that can hold many events. Better yet, buy a software organizer with an alarm system to remind you of your deadlines. The success of your business will depend on the quality of what you send out in addition to your ability to stay on track. Have a large sample book to show the customers you meet with, and offer them nice package deals to avoid piecemeal assignments that don't pay as well.

Start-up:

Your start-up costs will primarily cover the computer system (about $3,000) you'll need to maintain mailing lists and customer information. Expect to spend another $2,000 or so on advertising. Your charges will vary, but will likely be between $2-$3 per card. Add on a database maintenance fee to cover annual updates.

Bottom Line Advice:

Since mailing cards is your business, the best way to market is to use direct mail; send creative announcements to businesses on your "hit" list, inviting them to do business with you in the same manner you would extend a wedding invitation. The more creative you are, the more likely you'll be to win their business.

Expert Advice

What sets your business apart from others like it?
"I feel my company best helps businesses maintain contact with their clients and customers," says Jo Adamczyk, owner of Cards in the Mail in Akron, Ohio. She says that the most interesting and challenging aspects of her business are acquiring customers and explaining her business.

Things you couldn't do without:
Computer, high-quality laser printer, fax machine, and telephone

Marketing tips/advice:
"It takes time to build business and there is no profit while you are building. Networking will ultimately help you achieve a profitable customer level, as will sending cards of your own to potential customers on a regular basis."

If you had to do it all over again . . .
"I would better identify my target market. Also, I would offer complete packages that companies could purchase in order to bring each client to a more profitable level."

Handbill Distribution

Start-up cost:	$200-$500
Potential Earnings:	$15,000-$20,000
Typical fees:	$5-$10 per drop-off
Advertising:	Flyers or classified ads
Qualifications:	Marketing sense, time-management skills
Equipment needed:	None
Staff required:	Yes
Handicapped opportunity:	Yes
Hidden costs:	Spot-checking the distribution crew

Lowdown:

Businesses are moving beyond the traditional marketing avenues (magazine and newspaper advertising, radio spots, etc.) to develop less expensive, more effective alternatives. In many areas there is a return to a very old advertising method: handbill distribution. If you live in an area with a high concentration of people on foot, near a mall or in a large city, you can develop a handbill distribution service that forms a significant part of your clients' marketing strategies. You will need a crew of people to do the actual distribution, and you should carry out spot checks to see that they are actually handing each bill out and not dumping them. If all goes well, handbill distribution can be a very effective and direct marketing approach.

Start-up:

The flyers with which you advertise your own business are about the only cost for a handbill distribution business, aside from what you pay to your crews. You may need to carry insurance for work-related mishaps; check with your agent. Expect to bill between $5-$10 per drop-off or location; add extra for those jobs involving more time and effort.

Bottom Line Advice:

The simplicity of this business has great appeal. It's person-to-person, face-to-face. Creating a business that is an almost pure service can be very satisfying to those who love to make something out of nothing. A lot of your energy will be consumed in marketing your operation, however, and more will be needed to hire and manage your crew.

Herb/Flowers Farming

Start-up cost:	$1,000-$5,000
Potential earnings:	$10,000-$80,000 per year
Typical fees:	Usually between $5-$125 (from single item to large arrangement)
Advertising:	Ads in catalogs; signage in groceries and other stores
Qualifications:	Knowledge of plant growing, fertilizers, etc.; marketing/bookkeeping skills
Equipment needed:	Land, fertilizers, seeds, pots, supplies; optional: greenhouse, vehicle, computer, and office equipment
Staff required:	None at first
Handicapped opportunity:	Possibly
Hidden costs:	None

Lowdown:

Backyards, basements, or a few small acres is all you need to begin growing herbs. Americans have a good appetite for exotic, unusual, and healthy foods. Restaurants, groceries, and health-food stores are anxious to stock such products. Farmers' markets have grown increasingly popular recently, too, and herb growers can charge premium prices for their produce. Potpourri, dried flowers, and produce grown without the use of pesticides are also "hot" items to consider. Such a business is great if you want to get "back to nature" or stay in a rural area. You can also produce herbs and tropical plants in a greenhouse.

Start-up:

You will probably need a plot of land to grow your products; the amount you need depends on what you are growing, whether you wish to earn a full-time paycheck from your plants, and whether crop rotation is an issue. You will definitely need seeds, fertilizers, plant boxes and pots, hoses, and general gardening supplies, which can cost from $500-$2,000 to start. A greenhouse can cost from $500-$20,000, depending on its size and the materials used. You will need a vehicle to service your accounts, and can probably purchase a used truck for as little as $4,000. Business cards and stationery cost about $100-$400; you may also wish to purchase a computer and office furniture (approximately $1,500).

Bottom Line Advice:

Herb farming offers you many choices of products in which to specialize. You have the freedom of working close to the earth while still remaining close to cities. In addition, you can meet many others who have similar interests through the marketing of your goods. However, your livelihood is vulnerable to the weather and the seasons. You may also face stiff competition because of the current popularity of certain "trendy" herbs and flowers.

Herbal Products Distributor

Start-up cost:	$5,000-$10,000
Potential earnings:	$25,000-$35,000
Typical fees:	$25-$75 per herbal product package
Advertising:	Direct mail, networking, trade shows
Qualifications:	Sales ability
Equipment needed:	None
Staff required:	No
Handicapped opportunity:	Yes
Hidden costs:	Liability, possible licensing fees

Lowdown:

Health-conscious Americans look to herbal products as healthy alternatives to traditional medications, for everything from energy-boosting to sinus troubles. You will purchase a distributorship of established herbal products, then market them to a predetermined list of potential clients (however, you might have to come up with a list of your own). From sports-minded professionals to nursing professionals, your clients will cover a wide range of humanity, all with varying levels of open-mindedness to your products. Perhaps the biggest hurdle for you to overcome would be the negative, fad-like nature of the health food and herbal nutrition industry; you'll need to provide detailed information regarding the features and benefits of using your products as opposed to others with seemingly similar benefits. Don't try to sell your product line (which could include herbs in pill, tablet, or drink mix form) as a "wonder drug." Cynical consumers will see right through that immediately.

Start-up:

You'll need to put down some investment capital or make an outright distributorship purchase of anywhere from $5,000-$10,000. Most of your business will be through cold call and referral, so you needn't worry about a hefty advertising budget. With some aggressive marketing on your part, you could make $25,000-$35,000 per year.

Bottom Line Advice:

This is a hard way to make a living, unless you're lucky enough to sell your product to a specialty health food store and reap your percentages from there. If you aren't lucky enough to sell to a built-in market, you'll have to do it customer by customer, and that can take an infinite amount of time.

Home Schooling Consultant

Start-up cost:	$300-$1,000
Potential earnings:	$15,000-$45,000
Typical fees:	$25-$45 per hour
Advertising:	School boards, Yellow Pages, local newspapers
Qualifications:	Degree in education plus a teaching certificate
Equipment needed:	Books, teachers' guides, monthly planners
Staff required:	No
Handicapped opportunity:	Yes
Hidden costs:	Mileage

Lowdown:

Communication, organization, and the ability to juggle several things at once are need-ed in this field. Your job will be to set up the school curriculum and schedule classes for parents who seek to teach their children at home instead of in public (or even private) schools. You could possibly consult for a parent who doesn't want the child in the school system for religious or intellectual reasons, or whose child has to be out of school for a long period of time due to illness or injury. If you are establishing a new curriculum, you will need the ability to evaluate the child's skill level. If you are helping the student who is out for a long period, you will have to communicate with his or her original school on a regular basis.

Start-up:

Start-up is low (after you have obtained your degree). Be prepared to buy books up front and be reimbursed for them later. Charging $45 per hour on a regular basis could earn you up to $45,000 per year.

Bottom Line Advice:

You may need to join a national, state, or local education association program in order to get a job. This business allows for excellent, high-standard teaching without all the hassles of dealing with a classroom. You don't have to answer to a boss and if you find you don't care for the environment, you can quit. Networking is a definite necessity, but with enough contacts, you could find yourself with year-round work.

Horse Trainer

Start-up cost:	$800-$1,000
Potential earnings:	$10,000-$20,000
Typical fees:	$25+ per hour
Advertising:	Referrals from vets, equestrian clubs, interest groups
Qualifications:	Love for horses and skill in handling them
Equipment needed:	Riding gear, stable, horse trails
Staff required:	No
Handicapped opportunity:	No
Hidden costs:	None

Lowdown:

Riding is popular in many areas of the country, and all horses must be carefully trained to be suitable for this activity. A skilled, sympathetic trainer can make a decent living breaking horses to the saddle and teaching them to respond to their riders' commands. If you have the skills and experience necessary to consider training horses as a business, you probably have observed other trainers at work and can choose one as a mentor. Once you become known, you can depend on referrals for new business. Your days will be spent working with the animals you love and also teaching their owners to respect these powerful creatures to avoid injury. Therefore, you should also be trained in first aid when working with animals and people.

Start-up:

Costs are very low for this business unless you decide to offer boarding services, in which case you will need a barn or stables and paddocks. This equipment will run anywhere from $10,000-$50,000, depending on how elaborate you want to get. Charge an hourly rate of at least $25 to make a decent profit; your time is worth it, and the clients are out there.

Bottom Line Advice:

For people who love horses, this business can almost be its own reward. All horses need training and skillful work can greatly increase its value. For outdoor, active people who love animals, horse training can be a wonderful business. You may find that to make ends meet you will need to add boarding or breeding services. Horse owners can sometimes be difficult to please, and of course your work depends on something outside your own control, the horses themselves. This is hard work, requiring strength, agility, and a tolerance for bad weather.

Hospitality Service

Start-up costs:	$500-$1,000
Potential earnings:	$15,000-$25,000
Typical fees:	$10 to $15 per person
Advertising:	Personal contacts with bus companies, Chambers of Commerce, hotels/motels, local restaurants
Qualifications:	Knowledge of the culture or area in which you are operating
Equipment needed:	Dependable transportation and a stack of local newspapers, city guides, and coupon books
Staff required:	No
Handicapped opportunity:	No
Hidden costs:	Insurance, mileage

Lowdown:

Weary travelers entering a new city have literally no idea where the best of anything is (restaurants, shows, shopping, etc.). As a professional host or hostess, you could offer your services through hotels or local travel bureaus and would spend your days assisting those travelers with finding suitable entertainment or special places of interest in your own hometown. You won't necessarily get rich doing this job, but if you enjoy meeting people and like to show strangers around town or to travel, this is worth looking into. You can devise your own walking tours of the town you live in, especially if it is a large urban center, or contract with bus companies that need tour guides. Familiarize yourself with everything that's happening in your town; read every entertainment paper your city publishes.

Start-up:

You'll spend at least $500 on business cards to spread all over town (to restaurants, hotels, and travel agencies), but that's really your major expense. Charge your customers about $10-$15 per person, or work out package deals with hotels to help their own customer service efforts look even better.

Bottom Line Advice:

Cultivate contacts with personnel at the concierge desks of hotels and convention managers, as well as your local Chamber of Commerce. Even if you don't live in an urban center, if your area attracts out-of-towners or is known for something special, you can still make this business work for you.

Image Consultant

Start-up cost:	$1,500-$5,000 (depending on equipment choices)
Potential earnings:	$20,000-$50,000
Typical fees:	$50-$200 per session
Advertising:	Classified advertising or ads in women's or business newspapers, bulletin boards, coupon books, direct mail
Qualifications:	None except to be a good example yourself
Equipment needed:	You may wish to use a computerized video system to demonstrate what your suggestions will look like on your client
Staff required:	No
Handicapped opportunity:	Yes
Hidden costs:	Mileage costs

Lowdown:

How many times have you seen a misguided soul wearing colors that should only be on a flag—or makeup that dates back to Cleopatra? Did you have the guts to pull that person aside and offer suggestions on self-improvement? Probably not. Yet that is exactly what image consultants are paid to do. Particularly in the business world, people are concerned about the way they come across—and your most frequent clients are likely to be those embarking on career changes or job searches, recent college graduates, and brides. Your mission: to help them make a more positive impact on others through look and attitude. In some respects, you will be like the mother who tells it like it is: "You should wear cool blues instead of muddy browns, which make your face appear yellowish." If you are fashion-minded and have an impeccable sense of balance and color, you are likely to find clients nearly anywhere.

Start-up:

If you're just starting out, you really needn't invest in much more than mirrors, color swatches, and makeup samples. Once you become a little more established, however, you might add on innovative pieces of equipment such as a computerized video system that "morphs" changes on a picture of your client. A good place to set up shop in a heavy-traffic area would be a mall kiosk (carts can be rented for $300-$500 per week, but the attention might be worth it). Also, wouldn't it be interesting to form a cooperative marketing venture with a related (but noncompeting) business, such as a hairstylist or resume service? You could each offer discounts for the other's service as an incentive for clients to buy your own.

Bottom Line Advice:

It is fun to play "dress-up" with people who are in the mood for a change, but keep in mind that these people are probably going through some emotional changes that prompted them into action. Be careful, then, of hurting their feelings . . . criticism is easier to take if it sounds encouraging rather than critical.

Expert Advice

What sets your business apart from others like it?

Janet Neyrinck, Image Consultant and Certified Color Analyst in Akron, Ohio, says her business is set apart by the fact that it offers many services. "We're not just trying to sell makeup; our goal is to create a total harmonious image, including everything from dress and makeup to hair color. We believe in 'personality' dressing."

Things you couldn't do without:

"I need to have my makeup kit and, most important, my fabrics (for color draping). These are the basis of everything I do."

Marketing tips/advice:

"Be out there, be everywhere you can and introduce yourself. Also, be prepared to do a lot of research before buying your equipment."

If you had to do it all over again . . .

"I think that before I'd commit to one method or company's approach to image consulting, I would investigate all of the options out there. I would check the Directory of Image Consultants and ask others what's worked for them."

When to Hire a Consultant or Subcontractor

Your desk is piling up with unpaid bills, tax forms, and work orders. Your time is eaten up in the all-encompassing aspects of running your business entirely by yourself—and the work just keeps rolling in anyway. What can you do?

You could hire a consultant or a subcontractor to pick up the slack, help arrange your office so that it runs neatly and efficiently, or simply to offer you advice in an area where you are weakest. You can bring in such additional help on a short-term, per-project basis, by using the professional one time only or once per month.

But how do you find such a professional, and how do you know if their services are worth their price? If you're looking for an accounting subcontractor, for example, you might start in the Yellow Pages, or contact a local association for accounting professionals (they meet regularly and often have a directory of members).

You could also ask for referrals or recommendations from your own association members, as they have likely had the same needs as you and have probably used the services of a subcontractor at least once before. These folks will tell you everything you need to know about the pros and cons of hiring outside help, but be prepared to hear a lot of horror stories.

One way you can protect yourself against the false claims of a so-called consultant (one who is unethical or who really lacks the skills necessary to help you effectively) is to check them out with the Better Business Bureau as soon as possible. You might also do well to interview more than one possible candidate for the job: often, entrepreneurs get duped into thinking that there is only one real expert on a given topic and end up following bad advice rather than switching "experts."

One final way to protect yourself against harm is to request a list of references or testimonials from the consultant's clients. Ask if you may call any of these folks to provide you with details of how well the consultant worked for another company.

Hiring a consultant or subcontractor can lessen your load as a busy entrepreneur, but it can make your life more complicated if:

- the consultant isn't up front about each fee you'll be charged for the duration of the project
- the workload and estimated hours of the project are off in calculation by several hours or even days
- a "no compete" clause is missing from the contract, leaving your business wide open for exploitation by an unscrupulous subcontractor
- you simply cannot communicate well enough or agree with the consultant on key issues of importance to the project

Take the time to thoroughly check out anyone you plan to work with on short-term (or long-term) projects. You have the right to be sure that the professional has a solid track record and is worth the hourly rate you'll be paying. There's nothing worse than paying lots of money for a job miserably done. Remember, you have the power to keep from being taken advantage of if you spend a few minutes conducting a thorough check.

In-Home Mail Service

Start-up cost:	Under $500
Potential earnings:	$10,000-$15,000
Typical fees:	25 to 50 cents per envelope
Advertising:	Flyers and mailings to companies without in-house mailing services
Qualifications:	Knowledge of postal regulations
Equipment needed:	None (except for an envelope folder/sealer)
Staff required:	No
Handicapped opportunity:	Yes
Hidden costs:	Watch out for clients who seek to pay one flat fee and then dump extra work on you

Lowdown:

Companies who use direct mail in their advertising or promotional campaigns need help stuffing the envelopes and getting them properly prepared for the post office. If you're skillful at the manual end of this business (folding/stuffing/sealing envelopes), you'll be amazed at how much you can earn with only a few hours' worth of work. You'll need to market your services well—and if you find that you have too much business, it's a perfect opportunity to hire handicapped and retired folks who might be on the lookout for such straightforward, low-pressure work. Make sure you schedule your jobs realistically to allow for quick turnaround, because that is what will likely be expected of you from most of your clients.

Start-up:

You may spend a few hundred dollars or so on items such as letter folders and envelope sealers, but this business still shouldn't cost more than $500 to launch. Get the word out by networking with small- to medium-size companies; they usually have the need for others to help them on projects of this kind. Charge between 25 and 50 cents per envelope, and try not to quote a flat rate if you can help it; you may be taken advantage of after the ink is dry on your agreement.

Bottom Line Advice:

Let's face it—stuffing envelopes is pretty boring work. If you don't mind the tedium—if you can manage to do your work and still catch *Oprah* when you want to—this could be a perfect way to either supplement an existing income or build a modest single income. However, remember that your success depends largely on your own marketing ability.

Interior Designer

Start-up cost:	$3,000-$5,000
Potential earnings:	$30,000-$50,000
Typical fees:	$50 per hour or a flat, per-job rate
Advertising:	Yellow Pages, newspapers, networking with builders/contractors
Qualifications:	Some states require certification; you should be a member of at least one professional association related to this field
Equipment needed:	Swatches, sample books, catalogs, computer, cellular phone or pager
Staff required:	No
Handicapped opportunity:	Possibly
Hidden costs:	Getting set up with distributors and manufacturers' reps can run your phone bills up at first; budget accordingly

Lowdown:

As more people buy older homes with fix-up potential, there is more work for interior designers who are skilled at filling spaces with dynamic statements about the presence of a room. Do you read *Metropolitan Home* regularly? Are you addicted to the latest home fashions and accessories? If so, you may make a fine interior designer. But the work is more than plaster-deep; you'll need the ability to work with builders and contractors if a room is being redesigned with a specific aesthetic effect in mind. If you apprentice with an interior designer first, you'll gain much more detailed knowledge about the intricacies and nuances of this incredibly subjective business. Personalities are the most difficult aspect of the job—getting others to cooperate and work as a team with a unified vision is probably your biggest challenge. Keeping up with fast-changing trends is another. Still, if you like meeting with people and helping to create the (interior) home of their dreams, you'll enjoy the challenges and learn to overlook the difficulties.

Start-up:

Your start-up costs with an interior design service will be in the $3,000-$5,000 range, primarily to cover your first six months of advertising. You'll need classy business cards and brochures about your service, so set aside $500-$1,000 for these items alone. Set your fees at $50 per hour (or a per-job basis for larger work), and re-evaluate your prices after your first year of business. The more clients with prestige, the higher your prices.

Bottom Line Advice:

If you truly like working with people in their most intimate surrounding, this is the job for you. However, expect there to be difficulties such as timing (what if you get too many clients at once?), and clients who request too many changes and wind up costing you money. Learn to set some policies in writing ahead of time to avoid these annoyances; add a surcharge for any work that goes above and beyond your initial agreement.

Expert Advice

What sets your business apart from others like it?

"I seem to be the remedy person," says Linda Chiera, President of Studio Space Design in Akron, Ohio. "People usually come to me after they've experienced a problem elsewhere . . . I'm working on getting them to think of me first!" Chiera feels that her business is unique in that it provides expert service and assistance with complex projects. "We learn a person's work style and incorporate that into whatever we do for them, whether it be redecorating a home or redesigning their office space."

Things you couldn't do without:

Chiera couldn't do without a computer and CAD system, fax, phone, sample books/resources, tape measure, scale, and business cards.

Marketing tips/advice:

"Get sales training and get out there . . . join networking organizations such as the Chamber of Commerce, and if there's a mentoring program available in your area, enlist in it. Offer yourself as a speaker, advertise wisely (knowing your exact market), and hire seasoned professionals to do the things you can't." Finally, says Chiera, don't be afraid to make mistakes.

If you had to do it all over again . . .

"I would have been wiser about target marketing and advertising. I should have been more careful about selecting the right niche and also should have tried to become more comfortable earlier on about the selling aspect of my job. I'm trained as a designer, and sales and self-promotion have been a bit of a challenge for me until recently."

Creative Idea-Generating

You have a business problem (or opportunity) staring you in the face; now, how do you come up with a suitable solution or answer in a short period of time?

Try one or more of these tactics:

- **Mind-mapping.** You draw a circle with the ultimate goal in the center, and lines extending outward like a sunburst. On each line, you write down one possible way to achieve your goal. Often, you map out all the smaller details of each method—leading to clearer goal-setting.
- **Brainstorming.** Invite a few business friends (or, better yet, fellow business owners) over for an evening of pizza and brainstorming. Listen to what others have to say, even if you like your own initial ideas more. Their feedback might influence you later.
- **Learn from others' mistakes.** Read trade journals and business publications—or e-mail other business owners in entrepreneurial or specialty business forums on on-line services.
- **Go where your customers are (if they're not with you).** If you have a resume service, you might hang out in the resume book section of your local bookstore to listen in to what your potential customers are needing and wanting.

The important thing to remember is that there isn't just one possible solution; the value of thinking creatively is that you can explore many different possibilities—and if one doesn't work, you still have others left to choose from.

Internet Marketing Specialist

Start-up cost:	$2,000-$4,000
Potential earnings:	$20,000-$40,000
Typical fees:	Hourly rate of $45+
Advertising:	Bulletin Board Services, direct mail, trade journals, business publications
Qualifications:	Knowledge of marketing, business savvy, awareness of the unwritten rules and limitless possibilities out there on the Internet
Equipment needed:	Computer, modem, printer, fax, office furniture
Staff required:	No
Handicapped opportunity:	Yes
Hidden costs:	On-line time, time spent educating client

Lowdown:

Marketing is always creative; Internet marketing is even more so. You'll be creating the actual marketing approaches for a variety of different businesses to get the word out on the Internet. So if newness is your bag, then this is your game. Even more than with conventional marketing, you will need to deliver more than you promise, to tell more than you sell, and attract the attention of potential customers rather than push products at them. The Internet is the perfect way to inform people about some products and services, but it is still useless for others. You'll spend enough time developing your own markets, but once you do, expect to earn more of a cutting-edge salary for your toils.

Start-up:

The ability to create effective Internet messages will require increasing levels of computing power (equipment costs $2,000-$4,000). Expect to spend a pretty penny initially for on-line services, because you'll likely end up subscribing to all of them in addition to the Internet. Subscriptions to newsletters and magazines on the computer industry are also essential as resource guides—estimate spending at least $2,000 per year to keep up-to-date. You can charge $45 per hour until you feel you're experienced enough to command (and get) $75 per hour; you may decide to accept MC/Visa over the 'Net, so be sure to include in your price the surcharge for such capabilities.

Bottom Line Advice:

Experience, good sense, and highly refined marketing skills will make you successful at this new game. You'll need to be persistent in creating your own market before you can begin creating customers for your clients. You'll need a high tolerance for monitor-staring, and you'll need to watch out for the uncharted pitfalls that accompany any cutting-edge activity (such as time spent educating and rewriting).

Expert Advice

What sets your business apart from others like it?
"We're based in the fundamentals of advertising and design," says Larry Rosenthal, President of Cube Productions, Inc., in New York City. "We are also on the cutting edge; if it's new technology, it's been in here for an experimental run. Our clients appreciate the fact that we try everything out first."

Things you couldn't do without:
Rosenthal says he couldn't do without a computer and modem, Internet lines, software tools, and external peripheral equipment such as scanners.

Marketing tips/advice:
"Get yourself a home page, and make it a well-constructed, easy-to-use one with a clear point of view. Also, use e-mail to market directly to those who might be interested in your services."

If you had to do it all over again . . .
"I would have started working on the Web even earlier. I would've also e-mailed Mark Andreeson from Netscape and asked to work with him!"

Inventory Control

Start-up cost:	$5,000-$8,000
Potential earnings:	$35,000-$50,000
Typical fees:	$15 and up per hour
Advertising:	Business periodicals, direct mail, memberships in trade groups
Qualifications:	Inventory experience, excellent organizational skills
Equipment needed:	Office furniture, computer, suite software, modem, fax, printer, pagers or cellular phones for part-timers, business card, letterhead, envelopes
Staff required:	Yes
Handicapped opportunity:	No
Hidden costs:	Record keeping materials

Lowdown:

Your inventory control service is another of the businesses that responds to the needs of today's downsized corporation. Taking inventory requires many hours of labor that can no longer be wrung out of an already overburdened corporate staff. The work is outsourced to your group of part-time employees, who track and record the information for your clients. This business is a way of applying people exactly where they are needed, without having them on the client's payroll. Your ability to manage people and data is what enables you to perform these services in a cost-effective manner.

Start-up:

Work is done at the client's site. You'll need your own office functionally equipped for the management of people and projects rather than to impress clients. You'll need to produce data in electronic or printed form for transmission to head offices. Potential earnings could be around $40,000.

Bottom Line Advice:

The ability to convince business people to trust you with this vital aspect of their record keeping will be necessary for the launching of a successful inventory control service business. Higher-level management skills are also an absolute must. You must track person-hours, data, and client needs accurately and inexpensively to make a go of this type of enterprise. The potential market is wide; your challenge will be to reach it.

Jewelry Designer

Start-up cost:	$500-$1,000
Potential earnings:	$25,000-$75,000
Typical fees:	Some pieces sell for $50-$75; others for thousands
Advertising:	Jewelry trade shows, newspapers, jewelry retailers, craft shows
Qualifications:	Geological Institute of America (GIA) certificate may be helpful but not required; some formal art training and knowledge of jewelry
Equipment needed:	Vices, pliers, jeweler's loop, magnifying glass, molds, melting equipment
Staff required:	No
Handicapped opportunity:	Yes
Hidden costs:	Travel expenses

Lowdown:

For those who like to create intricate detail with their hands and have an artistic flair, this business could be ideal for you. Some people just jump into this with their natural ability; others who really make it big have had some formal art training and have also been picked up by a major distributor. In the meantime, hit the jewelry trade shows, craft shows, and antique shows with a vengeance and take a lot of business cards with you. A GIA certificate will be helpful with the respect that you'll have studied different types of precious and semiprecious stones and you'll be able to better price your pieces. This certificate also allows an additional income potential as a licensed jewelry appraiser; you could also buy back old jewelry and reset the stones in your own designs.

Start-up:

Jewelry has one of the highest markups going (100 percent minimum). So with little investment (around $500), a lot of imagination, and some smart marketing, you could be well on your way to a first-year income of $25,000. Try to get noticed by the press, and you'll nab more business than you can handle because people really appreciate having one-of-a-kind jewelry.

Bottom Line Advice:

Ever hear of the expression—"small but mighty"? Jewelry has been known to bring in thousands of dollars for a single piece. Here's your opportunity to cash in on your one-of-a-kind creation. Since not everyone's tastes are the same, you can create until you're out of ideas (which, hopefully, will never happen). The only problem with the GIA certificate is that it's a six-month program and offered only in New York and California.

Knitting/Crocheting Lessons

Start-up cost:	$100-$300
Potential earnings:	$3,000-$15,000
Typical fees:	$5-$10 per class
Advertising:	Craft shows, local library, flyers
Qualifications:	Knowledge of knitting and crocheting
Equipment needed:	Needles, thread, yarn, material, scissors
Staff required:	No
Handicapped opportunity:	Yes
Hidden costs:	Fluctuating materials costs

Lowdown:

Beautiful baby blankets, sweaters, and booties have an heirloom quality in addition to their warmth factor. After all, you don't buy or make a special, handmade blanket merely for its practicality. You choose such items for their sentimental value—and what better way to make a living if that's what you already enjoy doing? You could teach others your craft if you have patience and an eye for detail. You already know how much time is involved with each project and you can read intricate patterns, but can you teach others without winding up doing it all yourself? Marketing yourself at craft shops and networking with related fields will be some of your best advertising. Sell some of your work at art and craft shows to showcase your abilities. Always have plenty of business cards on hand.

Start-up:

If you are giving lessons, you most likely have all the equipment you need. Keep some extra supplies on hand. Have your students purchase their supplies before they come to class, which relieves you from making an up-front purchase. Plan on grossing around $5,000 per year; this would be a great sideline business.

Bottom Line Advice:

This can be a very relaxing venture to do in your home. You get to be creative and pass down these centuries-old techniques to others. Be prepared to hold class at hours convenient for your students, including weekends and evenings. On the downside, there is always the possibility that a student may drop out without notice. Try to fill your classes with more students than you think you need.

Lactation Consultant

Start-up cost:	Under $1,000
Potential earnings:	$25,000-$40,000
Typical fees:	$40+ per hour
Advertising:	Doctor's offices, Yellow Pages, visiting nurse centers
Qualifications:	Nursing or related degree; some states merely require certification
Equipment needed:	None (but you'll be working with clients on-site)
Staff required:	No
Handicapped opportunity:	Possibly
Hidden costs:	Mileage

Lowdown:

The womanly art of breast-feeding is not always an easy one to master for new mothers. For one thing, many of them are frightened by the prospect of having to be completely responsible for another human being; for another, many hospital professionals are simply not well-trained in teaching new moms how to breast-feed properly. As a result, there are many young women out there who are breast-feeding incorrectly—and quite painfully so. Your prospects look good for this consulting business if you are patient and caring enough to show them the way, and with hospitals increasingly being forced to release mothers and their newborns in a short period of time after the birth, there will be plenty of room (and need) for outside professionals. Your word-of-mouth advertising could bring in quite a few referrals, since many new moms like to share their positive experiences.

Start-up:

Your start-up costs are minimal; mostly, you'll need to make sure you have an adequate amount of resource materials and dependable transportation. For marketing materials, invest in professionally designed business cards—something that gives off a warm, caring feeling. Your fees should start at $40 per hour, collected at time of service.

Bottom Line Advice:

It can be stressful dealing with frightened new mothers and helpless fathers; you'll need a cool head to deliver this service. On the bright side, once you've accomplished teaching the mother how to feed her baby properly, the stress level will sharply subside and you'll have at least three happy customers.

See also: Doula/Midwife

Expert Advice

What sets your business apart from others like it?
Service is what sets apart International Board Certified Lactation
Consultant Barbara Taylor's Breast-feeding Specialties in Lake
Jackson, Texas. "I offer the added bonus of breast pump rental
services as well as one-on-one work with new moms. Also, I have an
extremely high referral rate."

Things you couldn't do without:
"My own business line with an answering machine; also, my own
office space in my home for professionalism and confidentiality."

Marketing tips/advice:
"Network with other professionals . . . being in a small town, I often
feel cut off. Most of my networking involves a long-distance call! Also,
you need to find out what mistakes others have made and share ideas
about how to promote your businesses as an industry."

If you had to do it all over again . . .
"It would be much easier to succeed in this business if I had been a
Registered Nurse."

Laundry/Ironing Service

Start-up cost:	$100-$1,000
Potential earnings:	$20,000-$30,000
Typical fees:	$10 per pound of clothes (this includes "The Works": wash/dry/iron)
Advertising:	Local papers, bulletin boards, flyers, Yellow Pages
Qualifications:	Knowledge of fabric do's and don'ts
Equipment needed:	Extra-large capacity industrial washer/dryer; iron/board or a professional press
Staff required:	No
Handicapped opportunity:	Yes
Hidden costs:	Insurance or "mistake money"

Lowdown:

Have some business cards handy for this profession and lots of happy customers to refer additional business to you. You should especially seek out professional women who simply don't have the time for laundry detail. There is no other business where word of mouth can make or break you as much as this one. You'll need to be a perfectionist and pay attention to every detail: people tend to think that the clothes make the person and if you make a mistake on their clothing, they take it personally. You should have a room especially devoted to this venture. Have clotheslines available for drip-dry, special laundry soap on hand, softeners, and starches. If you don't invest in a professional steam press, have more than one iron available, just in case. Be sure to keep all of your warranties up to date on your machines, since they are the lifeline to your business.

Start-up:

Overhead has the possibility to be low (under $1,000) if you already have the machines. Any washer or dryer in good working condition will do, but the extra-large capacity will cut your time in half allowing you to do more laundry in a shorter period of time. The large capacity also allows you to do big-ticket items such as comforters. Since your start-up cost may be low, you could easily make $20,000 in 40-hour work weeks.

Bottom Line Advice:

You either love or hate to do laundry. Since this is a home-based business, you still have time to catch a soap opera or talk show and feed your baby. Be prepared to correct any mistakes, even if they are not your fault (i.e., replace missing buttons, fix a shoulder pad, or totally replace the garment). For this reason, keep some extra "mistake money" on hand. If you make small repairs at no charge, it tends to be good for business, and the word will spread.

Lead Exchange/Business Networking Service

Start-up cost:	$5,000-$10,000
Potential earnings:	$20,000-$80,000
Typical fees:	$200-$300 per year per member
Advertising:	Business publications, newspapers, Yellow Pages, direct mail, networking
Qualifications:	The ability to organize and lead groups
Equipment needed:	You'll need to rent meeting space on a monthly basis (negotiate a special rate based on frequency)
Staff required:	None initially
Handicapped opportunity:	Yes
Hidden costs:	Phone costs; keep it short and sweet

Lowdown:

There are at least 5,000 new businesses launched every day of the week, and all of them need to connect with other businesses to exchange leads and helpful ideas. Your business brings these entrepreneurial minds to the table, encouraging interaction and support. You'll round up as many new business owners as you can, invite them to an introductory session, and hook them up with seasoned professionals. Then, secure a financial commitment of anywhere from $200-$300 per year from each member organization, and you've got a business networking service. What sets you apart from other associations (like the Chamber of Commerce, for example) is that you provide expert ability to mix exactly the right combination of professionals, allowing only one company to join in a given category so that there is no direct competition. You can also provide monthly speakers to inspire and motivate the entire group to continued success.

Start-up:

You'll need to advertise your service extensively at first; set aside at least $1,500 for this necessity (until your own networking members bring you additional business). You will also need to rent a monthly meeting place; check hotels, churches, and universities for the best rates. Charges are typically $200-$300 per business member.

Bottom Line Advice:

If bringing people and businesses together to work for the group's common good pleases you, you will be pleasing others and making a great deal of money doing it. Be sure not to invite any unethical businesses into the group; check each out with the Better Business Bureau. It will go miles toward preserving your credibility.

Literary Agent

Start-up cost:	$500-$1,500
Potential earnings:	$20,000-$60,000+
Typical fees:	15 percent commission on domestic sales, 25 percent on foreign rights, 20 percent on film rights
Advertising:	Listing in the *Guide to Literary Agents* and *Art/Photo Reps*; ads in *Writer's Digest* and *The Writer* magazines, networking at writers' conferences
Qualifications:	Should know a good book a mile away
Equipment needed:	Computer, printer, fax/modem, copier, phone system
Staff required:	No
Handicapped opportunity:	Yes
Hidden costs:	Insurance, copying, postage, phone expenses

Lowdown:

The literary life is indeed a glamorous one, especially if you're a literary agent. Imagine entire days filled with power meetings at large publishing houses, where you're negotiating for the best deal for one of the many writers you represent. You'll be offering everything from the right to publish to film and foreign rights (for publication overseas). Your business may also extend to book promotion, as you could negotiate book tours and publicity for your client in addition to the sale of the book project itself. Of course, you would hope to represent that one unknown client who could really score big in the publishing industry, such as Robert James Waller did with his *Bridges of Madison County*; look everywhere for talent—even in remote cities or small rural towns. No matter how hard you try, realize that not all literary agents can represent a Stephen King—and you should go in with an open mind whenever you look through the piles of manuscripts and queries on your desk. The successes could really surprise you.

Start-up:

Your start-up is relatively low ($500-$1,500) and mostly covers your initial advertising costs and basic office equipment setup. With your commission, you stand a good chance of earning a respectable income of at least $20,000—but look forward to making as much as $60,000 or more (depending on whether you get that "big break").

Bottom Line Advice:

On the one hand, you'll be making a good piece of change hanging around the best media minds in the business. On the other hand, you'll have to know when to give up on a particular project, even if it seems totally worthwhile. Often in the publishing world, trends take over and dominate what's likely to be published (remember, for instance, the Mafia book craze a few years back?). You'll need to constantly stay on top of what's hot.

Expert Advice

What sets your business apart from others like it?

Marie Dutton Brown, President of Marie Brown Associates literary agency in New York City, says her business is unique because her agency primarily represents African-American authors. "We connect clients to the publishing industry and provide counsel for writers . . . we focus on black life and cultures as well as books of general interest."

Things you couldn't do without:

Phone, fax, copier, computer, and typewriter.

Marketing tips/advice:

"Start small, think big, and follow your niche," says Brown. She enjoys the process of bringing an interesting creative project to fruition, and thrives on the positive publicity. She has been profiled by the Associated Press, and that has certainly been a profitable marketing tool.

If you had to do it all over again . . .

"I would have started with more capital. As it was, I started at home with only $1,000. It takes more than that to get things rolling."

Lock Box Service

Start-up cost:	$5,000-$10,000
Potential earnings:	$30,000-$45,000
Typical fees:	$35 per box (includes one spare key)
Advertising:	Direct mail, brochures, trade journals, networking with real estate companies
Qualifications:	None
Equipment needed:	Lock boxes, adapters, spare keys , tools
Staff required:	No
Handicapped opportunity:	Yes
Hidden costs:	Spare keys

Lowdown:

This is a highly specialized occupation; not everyone needs a lock box and your job is to be the best at servicing those who do in your area. Who are your clients? Real estate agents, construction companies, and anyone who owns a fleet of vehicles, such as car lots, utility companies, and car rental agencies. Although this is not a very common (or even obvious) service, it is certainly necessary and useful to have lock boxes that keep the wrong people out and let the right people in. Solicit your client industries in person and try to give them the best deal you can; if you can't budge on price, offer them the best service and follow-up care you can muster up. Build relationships with your clients to obtain repeat business.

Start-up:

Lock boxes are generally sold by gross units at $20 each; spare keys go for $6 per spare. Your bare minimum start-up cost will be $5,000, not including any advertising (add another $3,000-$5,000). With the right contacts and a good reputation, you could earn in the neighborhood of $30,000-$45,000.

Bottom Line Advice:

There are several obstacles you'll have to overcome to be in this service business; first, it's by no means glamorous, and second, you'll have to make the initial inventory investment yourself. After you have dealt with these two major items, you can enjoy the relationships that you build with your clients and maybe even get a deal on a new car or be the first to hear about the gem of a house for sale on the corner. Small fringe benefits like that abound.

Magician

Start-up cost:	$500-$1,000
Potential earnings:	$6,500-$20,000 or more
Typical fees:	Not necessarily carved in stone, but generally $50 per two-hour children's party, $300 per two-hour adult event
Advertising:	Yellow Pages, entertainment section of newspapers, bulletin boards, networking with civic organizations
Qualifications:	Ability to perform magic tricks convincingly, outgoing personality
Equipment needed:	Magic trick equipment, business cards
Staff required:	No
Handicapped opportunity:	Possibly
Hidden costs:	Advertising

Lowdown:

To be a good magician, you must have the ability to learn magic tricks and perform them quite convincingly (despite the audience's willing suspension of disbelief). You can buy kits from party centers/entertainment retailers or possibly take a continuing education course from your local university/college. Working as an assistant for an established magician is also a good way to learn the business. Having a good personality and the ability to work well with people is a strong selling point.

Start-up:

Start-up should be minimal depending on what you invest in. Visit the local library to find books on magic for an inexpensive way to learn the art. Investing in magic kits from retailers will cost you a little more. The most expensive start-up cost would be to take a class.

Bottom Line Advice:

Perform for free at your friends' parties or children's school functions to get exposure. Once your name gets on the streets, start charging for your services. Attempt to work with your city's parks/recreation department for leads or a convention center to get jobs at conferences. Working with an events planner or advertising agency is another good way to get your own name pulled out of the hat.

Expert Advice

John Henry
Magician

On Getting Started

To get a magic business going, try performing for your friends free of charge. Do some free work in hospitals or for community groups. Also, you should let prospective clients know that you're just starting out and practicing to be a better magician. That way, no one's disappointed.

You can also hone your skills and pick up tricks of the trade through attending conventions and meetings sponsored by professional organizations. National organizations like the Society of American Magicians and the International Brotherhood of Magicians are always a good bet.

When you're not actually performing, you need to keep up with the same kind of boring operations stuff any business person does. You need to get information from your clients, such as what kind of a show they want and on what date. You've got to keep excellent records and contracts. People are always amazed when I say, "I'm just overwhelmed with paperwork." Maybe they think a magician can just wave a magic wand, but my business is just that—still a business.

Maid Service

Start-up costs:	$10,000-$20,000
Potential earnings:	$35,000-$150,000
Typical fees:	$25 per hour or a per-room charge of $50
Advertising:	Yellow Pages, local newspapers, Welcome Wagon and direct mail couponing, personal contact with apartment and office building superintendents, and Realtors
Qualifications:	Management skills, ability to motivate personnel and improve their efficiency with superior products
Equipment needed:	Mops, rags, buckets, cleaning solutions, vacuum cleaners, carpet cleaners; also vehicles
Staff required:	Yes
Handicapped opportunity:	Yes
Hidden costs:	Insurance, workers' compensation

Lowdown:

This business can really turn a profit if you hire a crew of trustworthy employees. You can run the business from a desk in your home, if you have sales ability and the knack for managing others. Train them to clean efficiently, and you can earn a tidy sum. You might have to arrange for your employees to be bonded and insured since they will be working in other people's homes and workplaces. Always check back with the client to make sure your employees have accomplished the assigned task. Be willing to accept their feedback to improve your business. It's important to offer stellar service, because word of mouth will be the best advertising. Overhead is relatively low if you're not buying into a franchise—once you have an established business, you can buy cleaning supplies in bulk.

Start-up:

You'll spend at least $10,000 launching a cleaning service, but much more if you buy into any one of the fine, established franchises out there (they usually require an initial investment of $50,000 or more). Charge by the hour ($25-$35) or by the room ($50-$75).

Bottom Line Advice:

Make contacts with realtors to help new homeowners clean their house before they move in. If you do a good job, there's a good chance they will retain your services. Get clients on a regular cleaning schedule—but make sure you send enough people to do each job. Make sure estimates are in writing.

Mailing List Service

Start-up cost:	$5,000-$9,000
Potential earnings:	$40,000-$100,000 per year
Typical fees:	15 to 25 cents per entry (name, address, city, state, zip); about $1 per entry per year to maintain the list. Mailing out 10,000 pieces of mail could cost $800-$1,200
Advertising:	Contacting local stores, associations, churches, clubs, etc. to offer to maintain their lists for them, networking in business organizations, Yellow Pages, direct mail
Qualifications:	Computer expertise, fast, accurate typing skills, ability to meet deadlines
Equipment needed:	Computer, printer, specialized software, database, post office permits, business card, letterhead, postage machine
Staff required:	None
Handicapped opportunity:	Yes
Hidden costs:	Be sure to invest in backup tapes for your computer system in the event of disaster

Lowdown:

Although we all deplore the amount of "junk mail" that is dumped in our mailboxes each day, the amazing growth of direct mail is going to continue—and the opportunity to succeed in running a mailing list service for the companies sending those materials is tremendous. Start-up costs are low, skills needed are easy to acquire, and money is there to be made. Your service can include list maintenance, mailings, creation of lists, list brokering, and even teaching others about mailing lists. Understanding and meeting the changing regulations of the U.S. Postal Service is perhaps the most challenging part of the job. However, software, pamphlets, and seminars abound to bring you up to speed.

Start-up:

You will spend from $5,000 to $9,000 on the equipment and supplies needed for this business. Depending on your specialty, you may be able to begin for even less, especially if you lease a postage meter machine and some of the other equipment. Charges will vary for your services, but you'll need to set two rates from the beginning: a per-entry fee (usually 15 to 25 cents per name) and an annual list maintenance fee of $1 per entry.

Bottom Line Advice:

Mailing list businesses are relatively easy to start and to promote. You can have as large a customer base as you wish, rather than relying on just a few key clients. The actual work of creating and maintaining the lists is pretty routine, although it does require attention to detail and great accuracy.

Makeup Artist

Start-up cost:	$500-$1,500
Potential earnings:	$20,000-$40,000
Typical fees:	$20-$30 per session
Advertising:	Newspapers, beauty salons, bridal consultants, funeral homes, department stores
Qualifications:	Eye for color and contour
Equipment needed:	Makeup samples/kits, brushes, cotton swabs, a director's chair
Staff required:	No
Handicapped opportunity:	Possibly
Hidden costs:	Insurance

Lowdown:

If you enjoy making eyes for people, or just plain giving them lip, you will revel in the opportunity to be a professional makeup artist. Your services are needed in extremely diverse areas, from the life and action of the stage to the stately composure of the funeral home. You could offer makeovers for brides-to-be, new moms, college graduates, and those simply in the mood for a new look. Or, you could specialize in helping those who are disfigured due to accident or illness. Whomever you choose as your clientele, you will need to be familiar with all skin types and problems, matching your products carefully with each client's basic needs. With an astounding array of cosmetic products currently available (even at wholesale prices), you could produce professional and fabulous-looking results for just about any client in no time. Study facial structure to know where to shade and what to hide, and you're on your way to a beautiful new beginning!

Start-up:

Your costs are relatively nominal. Start out with some makeup kits and samples, supplies, and a sturdy chair for your clients to sit on—then add your brochures, business cards, or flyers. All of this should cost you no more than $1,000—but add a little more if you decide to sell the products you're using, because you'll need to secure a vendor's license.

Bottom Line Advice:

While you may enjoy the freedom and creativity of being a professional makeup artist, you may also find the lack of predictable income unnerving. Try to offer your services to groups to maximize your marketing moments, because the one-customer-at-a-time philosophy doesn't cut it with this business.

See also: Mobile Hair Salon; Manicurist

Mall Promotion

Start-up cost:	$500-$1,500
Potential earnings:	$30,000-$45,000
Typical fees:	$500-$1,000+ per project or a monthly retainer of $1,000-$3,000
Advertising:	Networking with corporations owning shopping malls
Qualifications:	Background in events planning, promotion, and/or advertising
Equipment needed:	None (but you'll mostly be working on-site)
Staff required:	No
Handicapped opportunity:	Yes
Hidden costs:	Travel (reimbursement may take 30-45 days)

Lowdown:

In the competitive retail sector, professionals like you are needed to constantly reel in potential customers with exciting events (such as bridal and fashion shows or antique fairs) and special promotions (discount programs for multiple purchases made within the mall). Although some mall promoters work as permanent staff at a single mall, you can make a business of working as a consultant to malls if you have the right connections in the corporate world. Meet with executives at companies that own several malls to maximize your earning potential in this ever-challenging market. When you do land the first client, you'll spend your days with a calendar, planning the best times of year to bring creative events and promotions to each mall on your client list. Then you'll work with the mall staff to ensure that everything comes off without a hitch; more than likely, there will be postevent meetings to evaluate each program's success or failure. Naturally, you will need to be able to work in two worlds at all times—both corporate and consumer. Having a keen understanding of what makes people want to buy will be your most useful asset.

Start-up:

This is a great business to start with little cash, largely because you'll be working out of your clients' offices and several malls across the country. You'll really need to spend your money ($500-$1,500) on self-promotion; business cards and networking are your primary ways of getting the word out about your services. If you have the right connections, you should be able to pull in $30,000-$45,000 in no time.

Bottom Line Advice:

Being on the road all the time might get to you after a while, even if you are a self-confessed "mall rat." Just remember that, on the plus side, you are getting paid to put together fun events that will be profitable for the mall—and in the long run, for you.

Manicurist

Start-up cost:	$5,000-$10,000
Potential earnings:	$15,000-$35,000
Typical fees:	$50 per set of nails (for length additions) and $15 for a simple manicure or pedicure
Advertising:	Newspapers, coupon books, bulletin boards, Yellow Pages
Qualifications:	Certification in cosmetology or as a nail technician often required
Equipment needed:	Manicuring table with a strong light, credit card processing equipment (if you decide to accept plastic), and nail enhancement or beautification products
Staff required:	No
Handicapped opportunity:	Possibly
Hidden costs:	Liability insurance and materials

Lowdown:

Luxurious nails are no longer for the rich and famous only—brides want them, society mavens want them, young women want them. You'll only stand to make money from this business if you are a licensed professional, mainly because there are simply not enough skilled nail technicians to go around. Often, the wait to have fiberglass or acrylic nails is two to three weeks (for reputable places) and you could potentially make enough money off of your competitors' overflow. At any rate, you'll be providing a timeless personal service for those who appreciate the finer things in life (translation: don't be afraid to charge a little more than you're worth). You'll create beautiful long nails that would make Cher green with envy, or you'll simply clean and shape nails for folks who are in the limelight often (even if it's only before a board of directors). Yes, men and women alike use the services of a manicurist, so try not to forget that in your marketing pieces.

Start-up:

Essentially, you'll need a good, strong table and a bright enough light to work with, in addition to your nail polishes and assorted nail maintenance equipment. All of this could cost $1,000-$3,000—but add on more if you're planning to rent space somewhere. Charge at least $40-$60 for acrylic, fiberglass, or gel nails; $15 for a simple manicure.

Bottom Line Advice:

If you like working with people from different walks of life, this could be your kind of business—hands down. However, the community gossip might leave you with information you'd rather not know.

See also: Makeup Artist, Mobile Hair Salon

Massage Therapist

Start-up cost:	$1,000-$5,000
Potential earnings:	$15,000-$35,000
Typical fees:	$45-$60 per hour session
Advertising:	Newspapers, Yellow Pages, bulletin boards, direct mail to corporations
Qualifications:	Must be state-certified (in most states)
Equipment needed:	Massage table, products such as oils and relaxing music (but corporate massage therapists work on-site)
Staff required:	None
Handicapped opportunity:	Not likely
Hidden costs:	You may have to carry liability insurance

Lowdown:

If you can't keep your hands off of anyone, being a massage therapist could bring you immediate (financial) satisfaction. Seriously, massage therapists are finally entering their own as certified professionals rather than as euphemisms for other, less desirable types of professionals. They must study human anatomy as clinically and carefully as a para-medical professional would, and must have the ability to make people relax enough to enjoy the service itself. With many of us leading increasingly stressful lives, such professionals should be welcome almost anywhere—from health clubs to wellness centers and even metaphysical bookstores. Many massage therapists offer their services to harried executives, and visit them on-site to work out the kinks in their backs and necks. Still others work out of their homes or in small, quiet offices.

Start-up:

If you decide to lease a small office, you can expect to spend at least $350 and up per month on rent alone. Add to that your massage table (about $500) and some relaxing music, soothing oils, and clean towels (allow another $250 or so for these). Finally, you must get the word out via advertising and/or direct mail to individuals or corporate clients, so expect to spend about $500-$1,000 on marketing, too.

Bottom Line Advice:

Working in a relaxing atmosphere while helping others relieve stress can be positively exhilarating for you—but it can also be tiring. Are you sure you can stand up to the phys-ical demands of this business—which usually leaves you on your feet most of the day? If the answer is yes to that question, the rest will, like tense muscles, fall back into place.

Expert | Advice

Elish McPartland
Massage Therapist

On Advertising

I think the most important thing is to have the right attitude of respect and care for your clients, and convey that to them. If you can do that effectively, word-of-mouth will take care of your advertising needs. It is amazing how a small group of satisfied clients—perhaps as few as five or six—can lead to well over a hundred clients.

The best thing to do is when you're starting out in my business is to give massages to a lot of people who have never had a professional massage. They will generally give you wonderful feedback, which boosts your confidence, and they are likely to become repeat customers.

Medical Transcriptionist

Start-up cost:	$5,000-$9,000
Potential earnings:	$30,000-$60,000 (billing 2,000 hours a year)
Typical fees:	$30-$40 per hour
Advertising:	Advertise in publications of local medical societies, direct mail, telemarketing, networking
Qualifications:	Excellent listening skills and good eye, hand, and auditory coordination, knowledge of word processing, dictation and transcription equipment, understanding of medical diagnostic procedures and terminology, good typing skills, impeccable spelling
Equipment needed:	Computer, printer if not using modem, transcriber, word-processing software, reference books
Staff required:	Not initially; may be needed to grow
Handicapped opportunity:	Yes
Hidden costs:	As many as one to two years of education may be required if you have little or no experience. Business cards, letterhead, envelopes are necessary to promote a professional image

Lowdown:

According to the American Association of Medical Transcription (AAMT), there is a shortage of qualified transcriptionists. This job is in demand for two reasons: many insurance companies are requiring transcribed reports before they will pay doctors or hospitals and transcribed copy provides health care professionals with the necessary documentation for review of patients' history, legal evidence of patient care, data for research, or to render continuing patient care. Since turnaround time of transcription is a primary concern for health care providers, increase your competitiveness by offering pickup and delivery, seven-day-a-week service, same-day service, and phone-in dictation service.

Start-up:

Computer hardware and software will run you anywhere from $1,900-$5,000 with a transcriber unit ranging from $200-$800. Do not forget that this job requires hours sitting in front of a computer; a good chair and desk at the proper height is a smart investment.

Bottom Line Advice:

Medical transcribing can become somewhat monotonous. You must possess high levels of self-discipline and focus as you work. In addition, the demand for faster turnaround times occasionally necessitates working nights and weekends. On the other hand, medical transcription work is steady and resistant to recession! This field is rapidly expanding with more work than there are trained transcriptionists.

Meeting Planner

Start-up cost:	$2,500-$6,500
Potential earnings:	$25,000-$100,000
Typical fees:	$40-$60 per hour or $400-$500 per day; planners handling large events such as conventions may get 15 to 20 percent of the overall projected budget
Advertising:	Networking with convention and visitors' bureaus, caterers, and travel agents; plan an event on a volunteer basis, advertise in meeting magazines
Qualifications:	Excellent organizational and negotiation skills; business background; communication and troubleshooting skills
Equipment needed:	Office and computer equipment, fax, telephone, reference books, business cards, stationery, envelopes
Staff required:	No
Handicapped opportunity:	Possibly
Hidden costs:	Phone costs could easily run higher than you budget

Lowdown:

If you like handling the myriad details involved in planning formal events and if you have the skills necessary to pull it off, you can have a great career as a meeting planner. There are many sources of business, from corporations and associations to conventions and trade shows. As companies become "leaner," employees can no longer be spared to handle meeting planning projects; also, meetings and events are increasingly viewed as great sales and marketing opportunities. Therefore, creative, talented meeting planners are in demand. You will need to be knowledgeable about many areas—everything from hotels to catering to travel. You may need to negotiate a block of hotel rooms, find exotic locales for company meetings, book speakers and entertainers, set up promotions, and handle the many small and large details that make for a successful event. In return, you may get to travel and stay at exclusive resorts and hotels, you will meet interesting people from many walks of life—and you will have the satisfaction of seeing people enjoying your event.

Start-up:

A computer and modem will cost from $1,000-$3,000. Software, printer, telephone, and fax will add from $900-$3,000 or more. Office equipment, reference books, insurance, letterhead, etc., will bring the total costs to $2,700-$8,500. Fees are typically $40-$50 per hour or $400-$600 per day. To get more assignments at the begining, you should do a few "free" events to give potential clients a good idea of how spectacular your meetings really are.

Bottom Line Advice:

Meeting planning can be very rewarding, but it often requires long days and hard work. If you are good at handling details, you're halfway to success already, because all those little pieces of the puzzle are crucially important. In addition to making sure you have adequate money for your start-up, bear in mind that a meeting planner's livelihood is often tied to economic conditions, since companies may tighten their meeting budgets to cut costs.

Merchandise Demonstrator

Start-up cost:	$500-$1,000
Potential earnings:	$20,000-$35,000
Typical fees:	$150-$1,000 per event
Advertising:	Yellow Pages, direct mail to manufacturer's representatives or marketing departments, networking
Qualifications:	Good people skills and selling ability
Equipment needed:	None (but you'll be on the road)
Staff required:	No
Handicapped opportunity:	Possibly
Hidden costs:	Insurance, slow reimbursement for travel expenses

Lowdown:

This is definitely a "who-you-know" sort of business; if you know a key marketing official at a large automobile manufacturer, you've got it made if you want to be a merchandise demonstrator at a big trade show for automobiles. Many "product specialists" (as some prefer to be called) can travel year-round to trade shows demonstrating products for one specific company, while others circulate their talents to many different types of product manufacturers. For instance, you can start as small as handing out samples at your local grocery store (of course, the pay for that is usually $25-$50 per day) or you can work toward establishing relationships with larger corporations in order to represent them at trade shows. The days of the gimmicky product demonstrator are virtually over, however, so keep in mind that today's consumers want intelligence and answers to all of their questions. You'll need to learn everything about the products you demonstrate by talking with everyone from the engineering team to the marketing department.

Start-up:

You can get started in this business for less than $1,000, because all you really need are some terrific self-promotion pieces (such as business cards and perhaps a postcard for direct mail purposes). Be sure to allow a few extra dollars for advertising, but really limit what you spend since your success will ultimately depend on how well you network. If you're a dynamo speaker and promotional genius, you can make a fairly respectable $20,000-$30,000 per year—and get to travel all over the country at your clients' expense.

Bottom Line Advice:

Travel gets tedious, even for the adventurous. You'll be expending huge amounts of energy up there on stage, and you'll have to work at sounding extremely knowledgeable about everything you show off. Get some rest, drink plenty of fluids, and be sure to collect an advance when possible.

Message Retrieval Service
(Answering Service)

Start-up cost:	$15,000-$25,000
Potential earnings:	$20,000-$35,000
Typical fees:	$50-$75 and up per month
Advertising:	Networking and referrals, Yellow Pages, business publications
Qualifications:	A pleasant, helpful phone voice
Equipment needed:	Computer with internal fax/modem board, word-processing and contact management software, phone headsets
Staff required:	Yes (usually 1-5 employees)
Handicapped opportunity:	Yes
Hidden costs:	Additional phone lines to handle more clients, personnel costs

Lowdown:

Answering services have been around for a long time, but the explosive growth in small service businesses has made them even more important than ever. You can take your pleasant phone manner and your good listening skills and create an excellent business opportunity. The latest software allows keyboard entry of caller information; pagers can connect you to the plumber or consultant who has hired you to be his "home office." A higher-tech approach is a voice mail system, with an options menu and the capability of recording and sharing long messages. This is increasingly a communications culture, and you can succeed by joining forces instead of competing.

Start-up:

Equipment required depends to some extent on the level of service you plan to offer. If you're using a phone system including a switchboard with headsets, you'll spend at least $2,000 on equipment in the beginning. If you opt for the high-tech voice mail system, you'll shell out $5,000 or more. At any rate, you will be billing a healthy monthly fee of $50 or higher, so the equipment, and cost of paying your staff, could pay for itself in a relatively short period of time.

Bottom Line Advice:

You have a pleasant voice and care about people. You know how to filter out what is important from the background chatter. No one is better at keeping track of things than you. What can we say? You're a natural for this business. On the downside, this business does tie you down to your desk and phones. You will also have to work hard at marketing to develop enough customers.

Mobile Book/Magazine Distributor

Start-up cost:	$100-$500
Potential earnings:	$15,000-$25,000 (sometimes slightly more, if the market is large)
Typical fees:	$3-$5 per stop
Advertising:	Word of mouth, ads in trade journals, business cards
Qualifications:	Excellent driving record and valid license
Equipment needed:	Delivery vehicle (car or truck)
Staff required:	No
Handicapped opportunity:	Not typically
Hidden costs:	Mileage (be sure it's covered in your contract), insurance

Lowdown:

Many local publications need to hire delivery subcontractors to make sure their distribution base is covered. If you find this kind of work appealing, you should have no problem securing customers, because turnover is often so high. Why is that? Often, it's because these publications tend to hire a staffer's grandparent or retired parent to make deliveries, and that person gets tired of the job because it can be a little stressful (particularly if the press run is late). You can set yourself apart from the rest by developing professional-looking business cards and making the rounds to different publishers, positioning yourself as a delivery professional and not just another flunky. The nice aspect about your work is that you'll get to meet so many members of the local business establishment, as many bars, restaurants, and bookstores carry the publications you'll be delivering to them on a weekly basis. You'll know everyone in town after a short period of time—and that can be helpful in ways beyond your delivery service.

Start-up:

Your initial costs will be low, especially if you've already got a delivery vehicle of some kind (a station wagon or small pickup can work perfectly). Expect to earn $15,000-$25,000 (depending on the size of your market and the number of publications you're delivering for).

Bottom Line Advice:

It's a cool job, with lots of independence and autonomy; basically, you're in and out of a great many places in one day. On the downside, you may have to endure the complaints of customers whose papers are late, but that isn't as bad as getting chewed out over a million-dollar deal gone wrong. Seriously, there isn't much here you can complain about.

Mobile Hair Salon

Start-up costs:	$1,000-$5,000
Potential earnings:	$30,000-$50,000
Typical fees:	Depends on the service (haircuts cost a lot less than perms, or hair color, but services can run anywhere from $20-$75)
Advertising:	Local newspapers, direct mail, coupons, contacts with nursing homes and hospitals
Qualifications:	Must be a licensed cosmetologist
Equipment needed:	Scissors, electric trimmers, rollers, combs, brushes, portable hair dryer, blow dryer, curling wands, towels, capes, and supplies (shampoo, etc.)
Staff required:	Yes
Handicapped opportunity:	No
Hidden costs:	Insurance, continuing education, cellular phone

Lowdown:

A cosmetologist who makes house calls? Without the overhead of a salon, this could be a lucrative business. However, you will have to come up with your own transportation such as a station wagon or van. Just think of all those who could take advantage of this convenient service—busy executives, stay-at-home moms, shut-ins, nursing home residents, and hospital patients. You'll have to figure in travel time. But if you plan to service a specific area on a set day of each week, you'll reduce time and travel expense. You can work with clients in their natural habitat; that can be very helpful to these clients and they will probably tip you well for your trouble.

Start-up:

Spend between $1,000-$5,000 on getting this show on the road, so to speak. Mainly, you'll be covering your equipment and supply costs (and, as a licensed cosmetologist, you can buy everything wholesale, of course). Charges will vary from $25-$75, but be sure to tack on your mileage in the fee structure.

Bottom Line Advice:

You might want to hire a receptionist or answering service to take incoming calls and book appointments.

See also: Makeup Artist, Manicurist

Motivational Speaker

Start-up cost:	$1,000-$5,000
Potential earnings:	$40,000-$100,000 (depending on the scope and appeal of your message)
Typical fees:	These vary widely according to experience level and your own personal magnetism; individuals will pay $100 and up to hear speeches they feel will change their lives
Advertising:	Newspapers, Yellow Pages, business publications, networking with associations (that always need speakers)
Qualifications:	Excellent presentation skills and communicative ability that truly inspires
Equipment needed:	None really; you'll be renting items from the facilities you speak at
Staff required:	No (unless you're selling tapes, books, or other materials)
Handicapped opportunity:	Yes
Hidden costs:	Travel expenses; make sure you cover these in your fee structure

Lowdown:

Dale Carnegie did it . . . so did Iyanla Vanzant, Susan Powter, and Barbara DeAngelis. They spoke to millions of people from all walks of life and business, and inspired them to feel empowerment, to accomplish things they never thought possible, and to win friends and influence people. All got their start speaking to smaller groups, collecting testimonials, and growing their speaking businesses to a national level through related book, tape, and workshop products. Do you feel like awakening the giant within you as a motivational speaker? Do you have a unique spin on how to improve oneself, or one's relationships? If so, your presentation should be top-notch. Study the many programs out there, watch how the other guys do it, then work every day at making your presentation better. Be sure you add value by telling your customers how much you can change their lives for the better—don't just try to sell them on a trendy, yet meaningless topic. Your ability to lift them to greater heights is what will ultimately lift your sales to new heights. Be prepared to travel—and consider marketing your presentation to any one of the larger seminar promotion companies. You might have to give up a piece of your profits, but it could be worth your while if they do all the legwork in rounding up audiences.

Start-up:

Start-up costs are very low for this business, mostly involving $1,000-$5,000 for advertising/promotion. After that, you needn't have anything else except a pager or cellular phone to stay connected to those who need you. As a motivational speaker, you can charge anywhere from $25-$150 per person for a seminar, depending on your experience level and the uniqueness of your message.

Bottom Line Advice:

Your business hinges on your ability to stay busy—plan to offer at least one speaking engagement per month to start. Organize your speech well, and videotape it for your own viewing before you throw yourself in front of a crowd. Get opinions from others, iron out the details, and practice, practice, practice!

Expert Advice

What sets your business apart from others like it?

"Mine is a high-energy presentation that leaves audiences with messages that they can use in everyday living," says Barbara Greavu, owner of Something Else & More in Canton, Ohio. "I present them with things they can remember in a humorous format that's easily understood."

Things you couldn't do without:

"I'm finally buying a fax machine. I have believed for the longest time that, if you have a passion for what you do, you don't really need much technology."

Marketing tips/advice:

"Read, read, read—anything and everything that's pertinent to your speaking business. You don't have a tangible product with this kind of work, so speak to other speakers to get the ins and outs of the business."

If you had to do it all over again . . .

Greavu wishes she had spent more time networking with other speaking professionals. "I would have researched better in the beginning, and I would have made a greater effort to talk with others in the business. They would have warned me or given me a better sense of direction, I'm sure."

Expert Advice

Carol Hamblet Adams
Motivational Speaker

On Getting Started

If you want to be a motivational speaker, you have to be able to choose an effective topic. I think it pays to be different. It's very helpful to ask yourself, "What makes me different? What can I bring to an audience that someone else might not?" Zero in on your uniqueness. Don't try to be like everybody else.

Make sure you have a good promotional piece on yourself for any client who wants one. You can start off with a one-page black-and-white piece that you can mail or fax to potential clients. Mine has endorsements on it from some of my clients and briefly describes who I am and what I do. You can also develop a brochure, which should include letters of reference from people in your audience and any kind of available press releases or clippings about your work.

Speak . . . wherever you can. And start off local. For example, Rotary clubs and Kiwanis clubs need speakers every week. Church groups are also a good bet. You should never lose sight of the fact that whatever group you speak before, you have potential clients listening to you.

When I speak, people always say, "Gee, can I buy a tape of yours? Do you have any books?" As a speaker, you should have a product. If you have a speech, you have potential for an audiotape or videotape. And if you go home and type out your speech, you have potential for a book. Begin developing your product as early in your career as possible.

Hooking up with a professional organization is also important when you're just starting out. Get involved in the National Speakers Association. Every state has a chapter. You can learn how to market yourself, how to develop better presentation skills, how to dress, and what kind of written materials are needed.

Movie Site Scout

Start-up cost:	$500-$1,000
Potential earnings:	$10,000-$25,000
Typical fees:	Usually a retainer fee of $3,000-$5,000 per month
Advertising:	Industry trade publications, word of mouth
Qualifications:	Ability to visualize; knowledge of general history and geography
Equipment needed:	Computer, cellular phone, business cards (but, of course, you'll be on the road a lot)
Staff required:	No
Handicapped opportunity:	Possibly
Hidden costs:	Passport; union dues

Lowdown:

For every beautiful landscape in a film, there was a site scout who searched for the perfect spot. As a movie site scout, you'll need to be well-connected and able to sell yourself to some pretty high-powered folks, but once you get one job, the others become easier to get. What will you do all day? You'll likely start by reading the script, doing a little research (especially if it's an historical or period film), then scanning the globe. Sometimes, it's just a one-shot deal, where you find one place for the entire film to be shot. Often, however, you'll be working on two coasts, or maybe even in different countries, to meet all of the script's required shots. The ability to visualize is incredibly important in this profession, because you are responsible for selecting the absolute perfect setting for a movie that costs millions of dollars to produce. Take into consideration the architecture of the area, geography, weather conditions, and people when selecting your site. A background in the movie industry would be helpful. This is definitely a "schmoozing" position, as you'll be forming relationships with people all over the world.

Start-up:

Most of your money will go toward socializing, since your business depends on who you know. Get your face out there and start passing out those business cards. Getting the job will be the hard part, so plan on spending at least $500 to secure your first assignment.

Bottom Line Advice:

You will likely have started in a lower position and worked your way up to this one. Hopefully, you have made a lot of friends along the way to help you break into scouting.

Multilevel Marketing

Start-up cost:	$500-$1,000
Potential earnings:	$20,000-$50,000
Typical fees:	Percentage, plus bonus for new distributors
Advertising:	Networking, memberships in business and community groups, direct mail
Qualifications:	Salesmanship
Equipment needed:	Basic computer setup, phone
Staff required:	No
Handicapped opportunity:	Yes
Hidden costs:	Marketing materials like catalogs or leaflets may become necessary, membership dues

Lowdown:

Some products don't seem appealing unless they are demonstrated. The classic example is Tupperware, which just sat on store shelves until the company realized that buyers needed to be shown how the top is burped to create a vacuum seal. Many other products, with vitamins being an outstanding example, are sold as Tupperware is, person to person. Often, a business starts when someone develops enthusiasm for, and commitment to, a product or company. The sales process for that product then seems to happen almost naturally. If you have recognized something like a line of cosmetics that is especially effective for you, or a nutritional supplement that has made a difference in your sense of well-being, you should consider participating in multilevel marketing. You will be selling not only the product, but the opportunity for others to sell it as well. That's what sets multilevel marketing apart from direct sales—here, you're aiming to maximize your own income potential by deriving percentages from other salespeople you recruit.

Start-up:

This is another business where you begin with nothing but your own energy and commitment (as little as $500 to start). Potential earnings are $20,000 and more.

Bottom Line Advice:

Do you know that you can sell? More importantly, do you love the sales process? Do you enjoy helping your customers discover products that will improve their lives? With this approach, you can make an excellent, if not wonderful, living in the multilevel marketing world. However, far more people have tried it than have made the easy millions that are sometimes promised. You really do have to work very, very hard. You can't give up when your first 74 efforts end in no sale. You will have to manage your time well, and you will have to find a company whose products are worth this much of your commitment.

Murder Mystery Producer

Start-up cost:	$1,000-$5,000
Potential earnings:	$20,000-$40,000
Typical fees:	$25-$50 per person (more if providing overnight accommodations)
Advertising:	Entertainment publications, newspapers, bulletin boards, city magazines, Yellow Pages
Qualifications:	None, but theater experience is helpful
Equipment needed:	Costumes, props
Staff required:	Yes (actors who can convincingly stage a "murder")
Handicapped opportunity:	Possibly
Hidden costs:	Advertising could get expensive

Lowdown:

Imagine, if you will, a quaint restaurant in the middle of Ohio. You and your guests are seated at a lavish table, complete with Victorian niceties and delicious food. You don't know all of the people at the table, and this isn't a problem until a dark figure walks into the room and begins arguing with one of your dinner mates. Suddenly, your dining companion is "shot" and "killed"—and you and your remaining companions must now embark upon your own sleuthing in order to solve the "mystery." Sound like fun? It should, because producing such murder mysteries is getting to be quite a popular business—particularly for those with backgrounds in theater. The challenge is staging a convincing enough murder to make solving it compelling for the guests. It's all in fun, and they usually know what's going to happen in advance. However, you'll need to provide them with clues (and don't forget the infamous "red herrings" that will occasionally throw them off the trail). You'll need to constantly come up with innovative twists and thicker plots. Feel up to it?

Start-up:

What good are theatrical events such as murder mysteries without sufficient advertising? Plan to spend about $1,000-$5,000 on this expense alone; then set aside another $1,500-$3,000 for costumes, props, and a good script. Charging $25-$50 a head for these charming little adventures could become profitable in a reasonably short period of time—but remember, you'll have to pay your actors something, too (unless you use university students in need of stage experience).

Bottom Line Advice:

There is a huge market out there for murder mystery productions, and it can be done even more cost-effectively if you work out arrangements with large local businesses such as theaters, restaurants, and hotels. Offer them a percentage of the take and you might be off to a more profitable start!

Mystery Shopper

Start-up cost:	Less than $500
Potential earnings:	$10,000-$20,000
Typical fee:	$25 to $50 per shopping experience
Advertising:	Personal contact with stores, hotels, corporations
Qualifications:	Knowledge of area to be evaluated, being a good actor or actress so as not to be noticed, being highly observant
Equipment needed:	None
Handicapped opportunity:	Yes
Hidden costs:	Mileage

Lowdown:

Mystery shoppers are used in a variety of settings: retail stores, typically where the owner is absent, hotel chains, restaurants, charitable organizations, government organizations, collection agencies, and banks. Their purpose is to observe the business from a customer's point of view and to report to management its shortcomings and strengths for the sake of improving service. A mystery shopper acts like a customer, observing the quality of the service, employee theft, plus shopping the competition for valuable information. Companies use mystery shoppers because they are less expensive than electronic surveillance.

Start-up:

You won't spend very much at all launching this one, but you probably won't become a Rockefeller, either—earning $10,000-$20,000 per year would probably be as good as it gets.

Bottom Line Advice:

You might want to stick to a particular industry where you already have experience or knowledge. Chains would provide multiple sites to shop without being known as a shopper, besides providing continuing business. Provide a written and oral report of your findings. In some states mystery shoppers are considered private investigators and therefore must be licensed: look into your state's laws regarding licensing.

Newspaper Delivery Service

Start-up cost:	$1,000-$5,000
Potential earnings:	$10,000 or more
Typical fees:	Usually a flat rate
Advertising:	Cold-calling
Qualifications:	Stick-to-itiveness
Equipment needed:	Van, canvas bags
Staff required:	Yes
Handicapped opportunity:	No
Hidden costs:	Maintenance, fuel

Lowdown:

You will be providing newspaper delivery on a subcontracting basis within a specific geographic area. With the move toward morning newspapers in many localities, it has become more difficult for newspaper publishers to find reliable delivery people. It is very difficult for the preteenagers who used to fulfill this role to get up way before dawn, deliver papers, and still get through a full day of school. You take over, delivering one or more routes yourself and hiring a crew to complete the rest.

Start-up:

You may need a van to pick up bundles of newspapers or to drop them off at your assistants' routes (could get by with just about $1,000 start-up cost). For a part-time job, $10,000 a year to start is easy money.

Bottom Line Advice:

This is another American classic: a job that depends on hard work (and an excellent alarm clock) rather than on education, social position, or good luck. You'll probably need to have others working with you to earn an adequate return on your efforts, and managing others always requires thought and effort. There's no glamour to the job of delivering newspapers, but it's good, honest work, and you'll get plenty of exercise.

Notary Public

Start-up cost:	$100-$200
Potential Earnings:	$6,000-$10,000
Typical fees:	$10 per requested service (average)
Advertising:	Yellow Pages, location
Qualifications:	License as Notary Public, usually upon recommendation of two lawyers
Equipment needed:	Seal
Staff required:	No
Handicapped opportunity:	Yes
Hidden costs:	None

Lowdown:

Notary publics usually add this service on to a related business. Witnessing signatures and administering oaths will bring you a small fee each time, but you will not become a magnate by this route alone. A surprising number of transactions must be notarized, though, so if you can draw in foot traffic or make yourself available for local in-town travel, it can be well worth the trouble of obtaining the license. Check the requirements in your state, since each is different.

Start-up:

Start-up costs are minimal, aside from the license fee and whatever your seal will cost you (not more than $500). A sign directing people to your location will bring walk-ins to have you witness their signatures. Fees are low, but so is the cost of providing the service.

Bottom Line Advice:

Why not? What have you got to lose? If people are going to pay notary public fees, why not have them be paid to you? Creativity in developing an associated service will enable you to make a business enterprise out of the enthusiasm for having things notarized that runs throughout American bureaucracies. Document typing is one possibility. Dreams of glory may pass you by, but the challenges are negligible, too.

Nutrition Consultant

Start-up cost:	$500-$1,000
Potential earnings:	$10,000 and up
Typical fees:	$15-$30 per hour
Advertising:	Brochures, ads in health-related publications
Qualifications:	Knowledge of nutrition and healthy diet; different states may require degree in dietetics or related discipline
Equipment needed:	Computer (probably), reference books
Staff required:	None
Handicapped opportunity:	Yes
Hidden costs:	Make sure legal and health ramifications are understood

Lowdown:

Nutrition is increasingly important to Americans these days—and most people are still not eating a healthy diet. Since people are seeking better, healthier foods and guidance in selecting them, you can learn about nutrition and share this information with others via classes, seminars, individual counseling, articles, and cookbooks. Nutrition consultants are also employed by hospitals, health clubs, and large corporations. If you enjoy helping and motivating others, this might be a great business for you.

Start-up:

Start-up costs are minimal. You can easily run this business from your home with nothing more than a basic computer and a minimum of office equipment. You will need to investigate applicable zoning and health regulations. Expect to spend some time and money on marketing materials to promote your business.

Bottom Line Advice:

Depending on which area of nutrition you pursue, you may need certain credentials (such as a degree in dietetics). You cannot instantly become an expert on nutrition; you may need additional knowledge of physiology, food, management, marketing, and psychology. One route to consider is the preparation of computer-generated, healthy meal plans for institutions. If motivating and assisting people in being healthier would be satisfying to you, this field may be the perfect choice.

On-Line Job Search

Start-up cost:	$3,000-$6,000
Potential earnings:	$25,000-$50,000
Typical fees:	$25 or more per hour
Advertising:	Home page, referrals, electronic and personal networking, Yellow Pages
Qualifications:	Human relations or other job search experience, extensive familiarity with on-line searches, ability to draw people out and help them assess their career goals
Equipment needed:	Computer with sufficient memory for high-speed operation, high-speed modem, on-line accounts, printer, office furniture, suite software, business cards, letterhead, envelopes
Staff required:	No
Handicapped opportunity:	Yes
Hidden costs:	On-line account fees, utility fees (especially telephone)

Lowdown:

Most people don't realize what practical applications the Internet can have for their lives, even if they have discovered e-mail and the Web Crawler. You can provide a valuable service to job seekers by guiding their path through the many on-line career services available. Preparing a resume that will be effective electronically can be a significant part of your service. The scannable resume, which focuses on the keywords that allow computerized sorting, is quite different from the graphically attractive resume on fancy paper that has until recently been the standard. When you start an on-line job search business, you are serving as the link between your client and a very large but invisible world of potential employers.

Start-up:

Computer speed will cut down on search times and on-line account costs (about $3,000 to start). You'll need comfortable furniture and a monitor that is easy on the eyes to minimize your fatigue. Hopefully you'll make at least $25,000 the first year.

Bottom Line Advice:

This is a new field, which can be fun and exciting if you like being on the cutting edge of the business world. It does mean, however, that your marketing efforts will be intensive and will have to contain a large element of education. The people who can use your help the most are exactly the ones who won't immediately understand what an on-line job search can do for them. Keep careful track of your successes to support your later marketing and sales claims.

Packing/Unpacking Service

Start-up cost:	$500
Potential earnings:	$15,000-$20,000
Typical fees:	$20-$30 per hour or a flat rate (usually $75-$100)
Advertising:	Bulletin boards at apartment complexes and grocery stores, classified ads
Qualifications:	None
Equipment needed:	None (but you'll be traveling to the client's site)
Staff required:	None
Handicapped opportunity:	Possibly
Hidden costs:	A good insurance policy can be worth a lot to you

Lowdown:

Today's society is an extremely mobile one; people move nearly three times as much as they did in the last few decades. With such a transient population, there are often no relatives or friends living close enough to the person moving to volunteer a helping hand. That's one reason packing services are becoming more popular; the other is that society as a whole is becoming increasingly dependent on "convenience" services (i.e., services that save them time or aggravation so that they can spend their free time doing things they truly enjoy). You will carefully pack (and sometimes unpack) items for the pending move, labeling everything so that each item can be easily located at any time during the move. Decide early whether you want to provide the boxes and packing materials to your clients; if you choose to, you'll need to make sure you cover the cost of such items in your fee.

Start-up:

For practically nothing, you can start a packing and unpacking service for the upwardly mobile. All you need are some flyers to spread the word—and you can place them at laundromats, apartment complexes, and possibly even at moving van rental agencies. Charge either by the hour ($20-$30) or by the job ($75-$100).

Bottom Line Advice:

If you're well-organized and know how to pack delicate items for often-turbulent travel, you would likely enjoy this line of work. Developing a system will help you manage each project efficiently and keep your hours down. On the downside, some clients could be difficult to work with—particularly if their move is due to a bad situation such as a divorce. Try to keep a cool head.

Parapsychologist

Start-up cost:	$500-$1,500
Potential earnings:	$10,000-$20,000
Typical fees:	$150 per visit
Advertising:	Yellow Pages, metaphysical publications, museums
Qualifications:	Certification as a parapsychologist (available in California and New York)
Equipment needed:	Resource materials
Staff required:	No
Handicapped opportunity:	Yes
Hidden costs:	Travel expenses

Lowdown:

Some things just can't be explained . . . but your job as a parapsychologist is to find ordinary explanations for the paranormal event. For instance, when there is a claimed UFO sighting or ghostly visitor in an old theater, you'll be called in to see if there is a logical reason for the perceived apparition. This is a skilled profession, but the skills are primarily of a higher nature; you'll be trained as a metaphysician (studying not only paranormal occurrences, but also the folklore and belief systems involved in mythology and fortune-telling). You'll need to know the history behind every supposed sighting and try to experience a re-creation of each event in the place where it has occurred; obviously, you're trying to rule out human intervention in such events. Many people are just plain weird, and enjoy making up ghost stories for the sake of gaining public attention. You have to weed through these folks, find the holes in their stories, and educate the public as to your findings.

Start-up:

Your start-up will be wrapped up in your certification and related educational resources (i.e., books on ancient history/mythology, etc.); you'll spend between $500-$1,500 (depending on where you go for certification; universities are more expensive). Expect to earn $10,000-$20,000, as your services are not always going to be in high demand. (In other words, don't quit your day job.)

Bottom Line Advice:

Okay, so your profession is perceived as a little bit flaky . . . but who are the folks we call on for explanations when there is no one else out there with a background in the paranormal? A "Ghostbusters"-type service would be a little far-fetched, but essentially you're going to be working around some pretty strange stuff. Still, recognize that there are literally hundreds of parapsychologists around the country today—so there must be something for you to do.

Parenting Specialist

Start-up cost:	$1,000-$5,000
Potential earnings:	$5,000-$50,000+
Typical fees:	$30-$50 per hour
Advertising:	Nursery schools, play groups, day care centers, YMCA, hospitals, bulletin boards
Qualifications:	Being a parent yourself helps
Equipment needed:	Good resource materials, i.e., books, magazines, tapes, etc.
Staff required:	No
Handicapped opportunity:	Yes
Hidden costs:	Travel expenses

Lowdown:

There was a time in our society when everything was passed down from generation to generation, particularly parenting advice. But in today's high-tech, dual-income families (who are often also many miles away from relatives), there doesn't seem to be as much time for history, or even for moms and dads to teach their daughters and sons how to be parents. Some new parents actually need to be taught how to be parents. Your job as a parenting specialist will be to ease their "parent-anoia." With the patience of a saint you will go into their home and teach the bewildered parents everything from changing a diaper to handling a tantrum in public and planning a birthday party for a two-year-old. Marketing yourself will be easy in big metropolitan cities, but don't overlook the possibility that your services may be needed in the suburbs and rural areas, too.

Start-up:

Your biggest expense will be in marketing yourself and keeping a library of up-to-date reference material on hand to help in unique situations. Since your start-up cost will be relatively low (under $5,000), in large cities you could earn an easy $45,000 in one year.

Bottom Line Advice:

You really need to love children of all ages to be in this business, and you have to be an excellent example for the parents to follow. When you watch a frazzled parent turn into a calm, loving, caring parent, this job can really be rewarding. On the downside, even though you're not Dr. Spock, you'll be looked upon as such and you should expect to be on call 24 hours a day, seven days a week. We all know that time is relative to babies and children—they often pick undesirable hours to have problems.

Party Planner

Start-up cost:	$500-$1,000
Potential earnings:	$20,000-$40,000
Typical fees:	Charge a base fee of $300-$500 per party or a percentage of total cost of party (typically 15 to 20 percent)
Advertising:	Yellow Pages, direct mail, flyers, referrals/networking
Qualifications:	Resourcefulness, creative ability, exceptional organizational skills
Equipment needed:	Planning system (hand-held electronic planner or a good planning book), phone, fax, camera or camcorder (to record parties so that other potential clients can see the results of your work)
Staff required:	No
Handicapped opportunity:	Yes
Hidden costs:	Travel expenses, spending too much time on each project for the amount being paid

Lowdown:

A party planner tends to all the details for any given social function—from hiring the caterer, florist, and musician(s) or entertainer(s) to addressing and sending invitations. Planners should have a creative flair and be able to suggest a variety of party themes to fit the occasion. For instance, you could come up with a Caribbean theme where all the party-goers must dress in tropical attire, all the music is calypso-inspired, and giant papier-mâché palm trees sprout from various corners of the room. Or, plan a party that is a surprise for your client's family members—with a little Sherlock Holmes-style caper for guests to solve upon their arrival. Whatever your plan, you'll need to be extremely well organized to maintain a good reputation, and since your business will grow primarily based on referrals, you'll need to keep this uppermost in your mind. More than likely, you'll put in way more hours than you should for each job, but the return will be worth it if your ideas are exciting or innovative and your execution of those ideas is first-class. In other words, do your job, and do it well—the payoff will be directly related to what you put into it.

Start-up:

It's a good idea to purchase some party planning guides from a bookstore (or borrow books from the library). Advertising costs will be your biggest start-up expense; be sure to get a Yellow Pages ad ($30-$100 per month, depending on ad size) since this is where many people who don't know you personally will be apt to look. You can charge either on a percentage basis (15 to 20 percent of total party cost) or a flat fee of $300-$500 per party.

Bottom Line Advice:

While getting started, you might want to plan some friends' parties for free. This will give you valuable experience and build a portfolio, so to speak, of your successes and innovations. Keep at least a photo album of your parties so that you have something to show potential clients. Nothing sells better than demonstrated success. On the downside, expect there to be difficulties in dealing with the personalities involved in planning a party. Remember, too, that your tastes (even though they may be better) will not always be the prevailing ones.

Computer Equipment "Musts"

Here's a checklist for setting up your computer system with everything you will likely need:

- ❑ A 486 or higher computer (preferably a Pentium II or an Intel Celeron processor)
- ❑ At least 640K of memory (but 2 gigabytes would be preferable), with Windows or MS-DOS Version 3.1 or higher
- ❑ A CD-ROM drive for some of the more innovative (and comprehensive) programs on the market
- ❑ Near-letter quality or laser-quality printer
- ❑ 3.5" diskettes for file storage and backup
- ❑ 28800 baud or higher modem; a 56K modem would be best
- ❑ An accounting program (such as Quicken, QuickBooks, or One-Write Plus) to keep accurate records and manipulate data to create reports
- ❑ Word-processing software (such as WordPerfect, MS Word for Windows, or Word for Windows 98)
- ❑ Graphics or desktop publishing software (to create your own marketing materials, slides, and graphs)
- ❑ Suite or network program if you have two or more computers sharing information
- ❑ World Wide Web Site construction software (if you feel like creating your own Web page on the Internet)
- ❑ On-line services or Internet launch software
- ❑ Mouse and mousepad

Patient Gift Packager

Start-up cost:	$5,000-$10,000
Potential earnings:	$25,000-$40,000
Typical fees:	Gift baskets generally start at $15 each but can run as high as $35
Advertising:	Direct mail to hospital administrators; flyers to health care facilities
Qualifications:	Some creative flair, ability to market yourself
Equipment needed:	Decorative baskets, boxes, glue gun, shrink-wrap machine, filling, ribbons; products such as toothpaste, soap, and lotion; delivery vehicle
Staff required:	No
Handicapped opportunity:	Yes
Hidden costs:	Insurance, vendor's license

Lowdown:

Creativity, organization, and the ability to visualize are all you need to have to make a go of this business. Build your market carefully—pinpoint hospitals, extended care facilities and even church groups (they often have members who regularly visit hospitalized parishioners). Who doesn't like to give a friend or relative a gift in the hospital, even if the basket just contains a get-well card and a few well-packaged toiletries? It makes both the gift-giver and the patient feel good. Gift baskets have caught on in the last five years, and this business is just a more specialized version. Most of your competition will be small shops, but even some of the larger retailers are doing it. Market yourself by getting in good with your local hospitals and non-profit organizations. Donate a basket or two to a local charity event to get your name out there.

Start-up:

The initial start-up cost is in the relatively low range (around $5,000 for supplies), and you may already have some of your decorative items lying around the house if you're crafty. What will constantly keep you going after more clients is the need to maintain a high profit level—this business will not be substantial enough to support you if you aren't constantly on the lookout for new business. Find the private craft retailer who only sells to vendors. Their prices could be as much as 40 percent lower than public retail crafters. Even though this business is still relatively new, it's hot. You could wrap up an annual salary between $25,000-$50,000.

Bottom Line Advice:

What a wonderful business to be in! Wouldn't it be a great feeling to know that what you are doing is making someone's day a little brighter, and getting paid to do it? However, this can be a very time-consuming occupation. If you decide to customize, be prepared to go on the hunt for specific requests. If you offer an assortment from which your clients can pick, make sure you provide enough variety. Don't forget—somebody has to deliver the baskets, too. If you can do it all, the better off you'll be.

Becoming a Networking Giant

Want to move to the networking fast-track? Here are some great tips on becoming a top networking professional:

- **Develop as many contacts as you can.** Add one new person each day, and you'll have met at least twenty new people per month.
- **Tell people the one thing you feel you do best.** Don't give them a rundown of all that you can do. It confuses, and even annoys, some people when the conversation seems one-sided; be concise about what you do so that the other person may reciprocate.
- **Become a host/leader, not a wallflower.** Show initiative; introduce yourself. Don't throw your card at anybody until after you've established a verbal introduction.
- **Cultivate your contacts.** Don't try to use the situation to get immediate business; instead, ask to meet privately later on. Nobody likes to feel pressure in social situations.
- **Extend your own expertise first whenever possible.** Be available to those who call on you for help when they need it.
- **Keep in touch.** Mail or fax articles that might be of interest to your contacts—it shows you were listening when you met them, and that you remembered what they said.

Payroll Administrative Services

Start-up cost:	$3,000-$6,000
Potential earnings:	$40,000-$60,000
Typical fees:	$25-$40 per hour
Advertising:	Trade publications, direct mail, networking, memberships in community and business groups
Qualifications:	Bookkeeping skills, expertise in payroll technicalities, taxes
Equipment needed:	Office furniture, computer, suite software, fax, modem, printer, business cards, letterhead, envelopes
Staff required:	No
Handicapped opportunity:	Yes
Hidden costs:	Errors and omissions insurance, software upgrades

Lowdown:

Supposedly the new accounting software packages make payroll easier for small business owners to manage. In reality, the drain on time and energy in setting the system in place is far more than the cost of having you take over this hated chore. You'll need to gain the confidence of business owners, which can be quite challenging, but once you do, you will have ongoing, regular business. As long as federal, state, and local governments keep making the rules and regulations more complicated, you will have plenty of opportunity to make a positive difference in your customers' lives. You'll need to be completely accurate and totally reliable. This is a business for the detail-oriented, careful person who just loves to see all the columns add up neatly.

Start-up:

Your office/computer setup needs to support the accounting/bookkeeping nature of this work (usually $3,000 to start). An annual income of $60,000 can be reached.

Bottom Line Advice:

Feelings seem to run high over payroll issues. Secrecy, accuracy, and just getting all the information you need to do your part all pose challenges. But the complexity of the task works to your advantage. Doing an excellent job may bring you referrals as well.

Personal Instructor/ Fitness Trainer

Start-up cost:	$100-$1,000
Potential earnings:	$20,000-$65,000
Typical fees:	$50-$75 per hour
Advertising:	Business cards, brochures, flyers, bulletin boards in health clubs
Qualifications:	Experience, physical fitness, knowledge of equipment and CPR
Equipment needed:	Membership to a gym; your own equipment if you want to do it directly out of your home
Staff required:	No
Handicapped opportunity:	No
Hidden costs:	Travel time needed to meet clients where they work out

Lowdown:

Do you keep yourself physically fit, have a great personality, and enjoy teaching others? If you answered "yes" to all three, pull out those business cards and start a personal trainer business. You'll have to market yourself like a pro—give seminars about being fit and cover the benefits of working out to get your name and face out there in this highly competitive occupation. Experience will be on your side. Remember, you are marketing yourself and motivating others to become physically fit at the same time, so you must also be in excellent physical shape and condition. Be prepared to work out right alongside your clients if they request it, teaching them all the latest ways to get and stay in shape. Keep a couple of before and after photos of yourself and others whom you've helped tone and shape. Do a video and sell it through local health clubs.

Start-up:

Start-up costs can consist solely of a gym membership; or, if you want the client to come to your home, you'll need a full set of equipment including free weights, Nautilus, and weight training equipment. That could send you into the $100,000 range for start-up costs. You have the potential to stay in shape and make a decent living in the range of $20,000-$65,000 or more, depending on how affluent your clients are.

Bottom Line Advice:

How many people can say that going to work relieves stress? Not only can you have fun and stay in shape, you get to have a social life on the job. Working out has become very social and everyone can do it, but the downside is, a client may quit without warning. Some people consider working out to be seasonal, so you'll really have to go out there and establish a good client base.

Personal Menu Service

Start-up cost:	Under $1,000
Potential earnings:	$10,000-$30,000
Typical fees:	$20-$50 per project
Advertising:	Brochures, advertisements in newspapers, food/health magazines
Qualifications:	Knowledge of basic nutrition and dietary requirements
Equipment needed:	Computer (helpful), nutrition resource materials
Staff required:	No
Handicapped opportunity:	Yes
Hidden costs:	None

Lowdown:

Most people lack a good understanding of proper nutrition, but they know it is important. They are also too busy with work and family responsibilities to learn about the components of a good diet. If you have a solid background in this field and access to a computer, you can fill that need. You simply create weekly or monthly meal plans, based on the specific requirements of your clients. Not only individuals need such services but so do hospitals, retirement centers, schools, overworked restaurant owners, and many others.

Start-up:

Other than the cost of a computer and advertising, this business can be started on a shoestring.

Bottom Line Advice:

It may be tedious at times to create brand-new menu ideas on a constant basis. You may also have difficulty selling your services to some institutions if you don't have credentials in dietetics. It is important to check out legal and health ramifications of any business that relates to food consumption.

Personal Shopper

Start-up cost:	$500-$1,000
Potential earnings:	$10,000-$25,000
Typical fees:	$20-$40 per shopping excursion
Advertising:	Brochures, classified ads, personalized notes to busy executives
Qualifications:	An eye for a great deal and the ability to match gifts to personalities
Equipment needed:	Dependable transportation
Staff required:	No
Handicapped opportunity:	Yes
Hidden costs:	Watch your mileage and be sure that you bill on an hourly rate rather than a per-job basis; otherwise, people may try to take advantage of you

Lowdown:

Do you consider yourself to be the "shopping goddess of the universe"? Are you able to consistently choose tasteful and well-received gifts? If so, this business could be your dream come true. Many of today's executives are simply too busy to spend an hour or two shopping for the perfect gift, so you can do it for them by offering your services at an hourly rate. You'll need to make sure that the client provides you with some method to purchase the gifts—or arrange for the items to be held for pickup by the client. Build a strong network of places to shop; familiarize yourself with every gift/specialty store, retail store, and florist in your area. You'll need this vast resource (and plenty of catalogs) to come up with refreshingly new approaches to gift-giving. Another part of your business might be purchasing items for busy executives themselves; they could provide you with a personalized size (and preference) card, then send you off on a buying odyssey.

Start-up:

Brochures and personal notes sent to managers of large corporations are a good way to introduce yourself and your services. Be sure to stress the advantages of using a shopping service (chiefly, the time-saving and money-saving factor) and be clear about the way you bill up front. Then, you'll need to start collecting catalogs, visiting malls and unusual shops, and combing the newspapers for sales. Your clients will expect you to know everything possible about shopping—so take the time to prepare!

Bottom Line Advice:

If you only want to do this job part-time for individual clients, you won't make as much as you would working full-time for large companies. Difficult situations may occur when the client isn't happy with the purchase, but you should be able to return anything you buy. All in all, the joy of spending other people's money is hard to resist—it gives you all the pleasure with none of the guilt.

Expert Advice

Mary Lou Andre
Personal Shopper

On Using the Telephone Effectively

When I first started my business, I had no idea how to use the telephone. It was so scary. When someone called, I would get very excited about what I do because I love it, and start to blabber out my ideas. I learned the hard way that once it is out of my mouth and I'm not yet billing for my time, I'm giving my product away! So I got a sales trainer to help me with a script for receiving phone calls. Now, if I get a call from an interested client, I book an appointment right away. I never walk into anybody's home or office not on the clock.

To determine my fees, I started with the Yellow Pages. I called everybody that was in my field, and asked them what they charged. I determined an initial rate at the low end of the spectrum at first. As I found out the extent of my talents, efficiency, and uniqueness, I gradually raised my prices.

I started my newsletter three years ago. My first mailing went to everybody who had come to my wedding! After that, I added in everybody that I worked with, and then new people that I met at networking events. That's how my business started to grow.

Personality Analysis/ Testing Service

Start-up cost:	$1,000-$5,000
Potential earnings:	$35,000-$50,000
Typical fees:	$125-$300 per test
Advertising:	Direct mail, human resource publications, networking with executives
Qualifications:	Background in psychology would be helpful (but may not be necessary)
Equipment needed:	Computer, standardized tests, a system for recording results
Staff required:	No (unless you grow quickly or have several corporate clients)
Handicapped opportunity:	Yes
Hidden costs:	Telephone bills will be high due to long-distance interviewing for corporate clients; keep accurate records and hold your terms at 30 days

Lowdown:

With the alarming rate of disgruntled employees suddenly opening fire on their former bosses and colleagues, it's no wonder that there are a growing number of businesses aimed at security and preventive methods. One of the best ways a company can protect itself is to hire a personality analyst to interview all current and prospective employees, determining their personality types (using a standard psychological test such as the Briggs-Meyers) and identifying their potential hot spots. You'll spend at least three hours with each individual, either on the phone or in person, and you may decide to hire on additional staff to cover several interviews at once.

Start-up:

Most of your initial investment will cover the cost of resource materials (and there may be a licensing fee involved for some of the tests you'll use). Aside from that, you may need to rent office space (from $350 a month) and place ads in professional publications (average cost: $500) to reach key management and human resource professionals in need of your services.

Bottom Line Advice:

You will enjoy the diversity of the people you interview, particularly if you have a background or interest in psychology or sociology. But the work itself is very repetitive, and could prove tedious. Also, making sure you always have more details than seemingly necessary to protect yourself from potential lawsuits later—after all, not everyone likes to be hired (or fired) on the basis of one professional opinion!

Pet Grooming/Care

Start-up cost:	$5,000-$10,000
Potential earnings:	$25,000-$40,000
Typical fees:	$30-$60 per pet-primping session
Advertising:	Yellow Pages, direct mail, community bulletin boards, referrals from vets
Qualifications:	Experience, patience, knowledge of animal behavior patterns, familiarity with the grooming standards of different breeds
Equipment needed:	Grooming table, clippers, brushes, combs, bathing tub/shower accessories, shampoos, dryer, detangler, hair bows, business card
Staff required:	No
Handicapped opportunity:	No
Hidden costs:	Supplies could get out of hand

Lowdown:

You have to really love animals to consider this business. But if you enjoy working with pets—many of whom may not enjoy taking a bath—you can build a decent business providing these services. Pet ownership increases each year in this country, but people have less free time than ever. What Afghan owners can really manage to comb out their pet's entire coat every day, as the books recommend? The popular white poodles need considerable grooming to present themselves in a clean, fluffy, well-trimmed coat. Aside from the pet's appearance, good health practices dictate cleaning and brushing the coat regularly. Once you establish rapport with Rover, you are likely to have regular repeat business from his owner. Giving cats their flea baths is another popular service (to the owner, definitely not to the feline). As an add-on, consider selling pet supplies and/or specialty products for the pampered pet.

Start-up:

Trying to do all this one dog at a time in your family bathtub is a poor idea. To make a go of the business, you'll need the setting and equipment to do a professional job without breaking your back even if it is in your home. This may set you back around $10,000, but you stand a good chance of earning it all back in a year or so if there aren't many competitors in your area. Charge between $30-$60, depending on whether you're in the country or in a large city.

Bottom Line Advice:

You may not be the only pet grooming service in your community, but you can be the best. You can offer pickup and delivery services, you can specialize in terrier coat stripping or caring for poodles, you can leave each "patient" happy and sweet-smelling. You'll need to make your customers feel that your service is the one that they can't live without. This is hard, physical work, but each grooming session leaves a beloved pet looking better—until he or she can get outside again.

Pollster

Start-up cost:	$1,000-1,500
Potential earnings:	$15,000-$40,000
Typical fees:	$10-$20 per hour or a flat rate of $150 and up
Advertising:	Connections, referrals, networking, newspaper ads
Qualifications:	Energy, patience, people skills
Equipment needed:	Computer, office suite software, printer, office furniture, business cards, phone
Staff required:	Yes (1-2 people)
Handicapped opportunity:	No
Hidden costs:	Time is money, so plan well

Lowdown:

To become a pollster you will need an ability to get people to talk to you. You can take your energy, your determination to keep going in the face of rejection, and your genuine interest in what people have to say and turn this into a business. Constructing the questions to ask is one of the jobs of a pollster. Another may be finding the right people to carry out polls devised by someone else. Typically pollsters focus on one geographic or demographic area.

Start-up:

You can probably make do with very little equipment to start but will be able to produce more professional-looking reports with a computer and printer. Tabulating results will be much easier with a good spreadsheet program (around $100-$300). Charge by the hour ($10-$20 per) when you can, because this is a time-consuming business. If your client wants to pay a flat fee, a good starting point is $150.

Bottom Line Advice:

This can be a fascinating field. You will be gathering and analyzing information that can be gleaned no other way. But marketing your services will be extremely challenging. Polling requires connections in government as well as industry, so your marketing skills need to be top-drawer. Your network will lead you to further referrals. Be careful; this business ebbs and flows depending on the electoral season, the weather, and other factors out of your control.

Private Tutor

Start-up cost:	$500
Potential earnings:	$15,000-$20,000
Typical fees:	$10-$20 per hour
Advertising:	Classified ads, Yellow Pages, word of mouth (school principals would be a good group to network with)
Qualifications:	Teaching experience or degree in area of expertise
Equipment needed:	None
Staff required:	None
Handicapped opportunity:	Yes
Hidden costs:	Watch your mileage

Lowdown:

Since classrooms are getting larger and larger, many students' needs are getting over-looked. Your services may be needed to bring a struggling student up to speed—and the best part about this type of business is that it is recession-proof! As long as there are students, there will be a strong need for capable individuals to guide them to scholastic success. Determine where your area of expertise lies (is it in history? English? mathematics?) and meet with teachers in this subject to ask for referrals. Once you get a few clients, your word of mouth will grow quickly, and you may find that you need to network with other tutors to build referral systems of your own. At any rate, as a tutor you will find out the students' needs (probably in a written report from their teacher) and develop lesson plans tailored to that specific need. The opportunity to be creative is up to you, so try to make the lessons interesting and empower the student so that each success feels like his or her own.

Start-up:

Purchase a few used textbooks (preferably with teacher's guides) and buy yourself some good books on learning challenges and motivation to succeed. To be a good inspiration to your student, you'll need to demonstrate your own willingness to learn. Your only other start-up cost will be advertising, and that will generally stay under $500.

Bottom Line Advice:

Encouraging a young student's success while fostering a thirst for knowledge can be richly rewarding if you are genuinely interested in education. Helping a student over-come what seemed like an obstacle offers you—and the rest of the world—optimism about our own possibilities. Aside from an occasional obnoxious child, what's there to hate about that?

Professional Organizer

Start-up cost:	$500-$1,000
Potential earnings:	$25,000-$45,000
Typical fees:	$25-$40 per hour
Advertising:	Write articles for your local newspapers on time management and organizing space, Welcome Wagon, direct mail coupons; conduct seminars through local community continuing education; network
Qualifications:	You must be a highly organized person by nature, with drive for efficiency; knowledge of systems, furniture, products, supplies and accessories are a must
Equipment:	Pager or cellular phone, computers
Staff:	No
Handicapped opportunity:	No
Hidden costs:	Mileage and cellular phone bills

Lowdown:

Most organizers specialize in one of five areas: space planning (organizing office arrangement of furniture, traffic, lighting, noise, and leisure space); time management (setting goals, developing action plans, scheduling, and delegating tasks); paper management (organizing the steady flow of information materials by setting up filing and retrieval systems, sometimes with the aid of a computer); clutter control (finding the proper and efficient placement for things to keep clutter to a minimum); closet/storage design (organizing closet and storage space). Choose one or two and market your services accordingly. This business would thrive in highly urban areas with busy professionals who want their home life to run as smoothly as the office—and it's much more fun to organize other people's lives than to run our own.

Start-up:

You'll spend at least $500 or so on business cards for networking—but that's almost negligible considering that you'll be charging $25-$45 per hour for your expertise.

Bottom Line Advice:

Look into the National Association of Professional Organizers for more information. Hook up with an organization that conducts seminars, and offer your services as an instructor. This can supplement the income of your consulting service rather nicely.

Public Relations

Start-up cost:	$5,000-$10,000
Potential earnings:	$35,000-$75,000
Typical fees:	$50-$75 per hour, a bid-per-job basis, or monthly retainer
Advertising:	Networking and personal contacts, speeches before business or community groups, volunteer work for nonprofit organizations, telemarketing
Qualifications:	Strong communication and telephone skills, assertiveness and persuasiveness, ability to deal effectively with abstract concepts, high energy level
Equipment needed:	Computer with modem, printer, and fax, desktop publishing software, telephone headset, multiple phone lines with call-forwarding and conferencing features, office furniture, business card, letterhead, envelopes
Staff required:	No
Handicapped opportunity:	Yes
Hidden costs:	Slow starting time; expect two years before profit

Lowdown:

As with so many other fields, the demand for PR is growing. At the same time, corporations are cutting their public relations staffs (usually the first to go in the age of downsizing). The work is definitely being farmed out, so public relations is ideal for a home-based business. Relationships with clients take time to develop, though, and depend in part on your network of contacts in the media. When a small company has a breakthrough new product, when advertising is too expensive, when an organization needs to get its message across to the public, or when a negative situation occurs that needs a positive spin, your PR services can be invaluable. To attract media attention and interest, you will need outstanding writing and speaking skills, a healthy dose of creativity, awareness of what the different types of media (trade journals, the nightly news shows) are hungry for, and an ability to put all the pieces together. It's fun, yet tough to do well unless you're an animal at networking with influential media types.

Start-up:

A very well-equipped office is a must, and you will need to present yourself and your business at the level of polish and professionalism you are selling for your clients. Expect to spend at least $4,000 on your office and equipment; bill at least $50-$75 per hour for your expertise.

Bottom Line Advice:

For creative, dynamic, and above all energetic people, public relations is a wonderful field. If you thrive on relationships with many different individuals and organizations and love the stimulation of constant change, you should consider making PR your business.

As a solo practitioner, you'll start with small projects and gradually expand your network and contacts to take on more complex projects. Not everyone has the skills and attributes to make a success of PR, although many people are out there trying. You will need to produce results; recognize that your business will take tremendous time and effort to grow. Marketing your own services must be a priority even as you complete one project after another for your clients. Media representatives can be fickle; getting publicity for your clients will require new angles and ideas each time to catch the media's attention.

Expert Advice

What sets your business apart from others like it?
Eric Yaverbaum, President of the New York City-based Jericho Promotions, says his soaring public relations business is unique because of how often the company itself is in the press. "We're on national TV regularly, and we've been written about in the Wall Street Journal. Our customers know we're in a league of our own in terms of creativity."

Things you couldn't do without:
Yaverbaum says he couldn't do without a fax machine, mailing list database, multiple phone lines, and E-mail.

Marketing tips/advice:
"Hire the right people to establish credibility . . . you're buying their experience and capitalizing on it. Doing that has saved me at least ten years of pounding the pavement. Also, when you lose someone, you can turn it into an opportunity to bring in new business. One of my people moved to a company that later became a client as a result of my professionalism in the matter."

If you had to do it all over again . . .
"I probably wouldn't do it . . . starting a business is a tough road for anyone. I guess I liked it best when the company was small enough to have a lot of fun."

Rare Book Dealer/
Search Service

Start-up cost:	$5,000-$10,000
Potential earnings:	$20,000-$40,000
Typical fees:	$10-$15 plus a percentage of sale on book (based on your markup)
Advertising:	Yellow Pages, book industry publications, referrals from bookstores
Qualifications:	Good organizational skills and excellent follow-up ability
Equipment needed:	Computer, printer, fax/modem, phone with 800 number, on-line services
Staff required:	No
Handicapped opportunity:	Yes
Hidden costs:	On-line services and phone bills

Lowdown:

Some avid readers will go to extraordinary lengths to find a used or rare book that they'd relish having in their private collection. Whether you're providing this service in addition to running a bookstore (as many searchers do) or running it as a separate business, you'll need to be highly detail-oriented and well-organized to make this business profitable. The good news is, there are plenty of publications that you can subscribe to, and these provide monthly listings of what books are currently available through other dealers. Sometimes, you'll be lucky enough to work out an even trade (and maximize your own profit on the book you're selling to the customer). Most often, however, you'll derive your income from a search fee ($10-$15 in some areas) and a sales commission on the book itself (which you will have priced accordingly to suit your bank account's needs). The older and more rare the book, the harder it is to locate—but if you can manage to drum up one yellow-paged copy, your earnings could be quite high on just one book.

Start-up:

It will take between $5,000-$10,000 to get you started with your computer and on-line searches; expect to spend $1,000 or so on advertising in your first year. If you are good at what you do, you can see income potentials of $20,000-$40,000 per year.

Bottom Line Advice:

The stress level is actually quite low in this field, and you can pretty much search for a book at your own pace. However, you don't get paid as much for looking as you do for finding—so use computer on-line services to expedite your searches.

Recreational Coupon Distributor

Start-up cost:	$5,000-$10,000
Potential earnings:	$15,000-$35,000
Typical fees:	Advertising rates vary from $150-$3,000 per client
Advertising:	Yellow Pages, direct mail to recreational facilities, health clubs
Qualifications:	Good organizational skills
Equipment needed:	Computer with desktop publishing software, laser printer, stationery and rate cards/contracts, perhaps a delivery vehicle
Staff required:	No (but you may want to get some commission-only salespeople and hire someone to distribute for you)
Handicapped opportunity:	Possibly
Hidden costs:	Printing and paper costs are skyrocketing; keep a watchful eye to make sure your rates cover costs

Lowdown:

Everyone likes to have a good time—and everyone likes a good deal, too. That's why coupon books for recreational activities are such sure bets; they'll be read, kept, and used better than any other kind of coupon (except food coupons, of course). Your mission is to sell those in the recreation industry on giving some of their advertising dollars to you—then to make sure that your package is enticing enough to gain the interest of potential customers. If you produce the coupon books too cheaply, they'll get tossed like any other piece of junk mail; spend some money on a decent desktop publishing system that allows you to create your own innovative ads, then work with printers to get the best deals on paper and printing costs. Ask your printer early in the process how to best save money; familiarize yourself with the printing process so that you have a clear understanding of how and where you can save. Plan your distribution system well, and count on hiring at least one person to distribute. You won't have the time to do it all yourself.

Start-up:

You should be able to stay in the $5,000-$10,000 range to get this business off the ground; primarily, you'll be spending it on your computer system and travel/mileage or phone expenses you'll incur in trying to build sales. However, if you work hard and don't mind putting in lots of long hours, you could make $15,000-$35,000 or more at this one.

Bottom Line Advice:

Your business will hinge on your reputation; you might want to join your local Chamber of Commerce for networking and credibility purposes, or become active in other community organizations.

Referral Service

Start-up cost:	$3,000-$5,000
Potential earnings:	$5,000-$40,000, depending on experience level
Typical fees:	Varied according to type of service
Advertising:	Yellow Pages, newspapers, bulletin boards
Qualifications:	None
Equipment needed:	Phone, computer with extensive database of businesses
Staff required:	No
Handicapped opportunity:	Yes
Hidden costs:	Updating your database annually will cost you some money

Lowdown:

How many times have you been stuck in the middle of nowhere with absolutely no idea who to call for what you need? A referral service eliminates the time you'd spend thumbing through every category in the Yellow Pages, not knowing who is reputable and who is not. With one phone call, a referral service can locate all of the reputable businesses in any given category and within a specific geographic area. As a referral service operator, you would gather every piece of information about these companies, perhaps aligning yourself closely to Chambers of Commerce or the Better Business Bureau to ensure the credibility of each company you refer. You may work out a commission with the companies you represent, or you may set up an on-line service or 900-number for folks in need of referrals so that you can earn income from them. Some referral services do a combination of the two methods. At any rate, you'll need to establish yourself as an authority on a wide variety of businesses, so research is vital to success.

Start-up:

Expect to spend anywhere from $3,000-$5,000 on computer and related databases to keep your research time down to a minimum. On-line services, the phone book, and bulletin boards provide you with various avenues of income; your fees will depend on which method(s) you choose.

Bottom Line Advice:

If you don't mind dealing with people and vast amounts of data, and if you're skilled in matching the two, you'll likely succeed in this business. However, unless people know about you, they won't call . . . be sure to advertise in the most high-profile places you can afford.

Relocation Consultant

Start-up cost:	$3,000-$6,000
Potential earnings:	$15,000 and more
Typical fees:	$25-$35 per hour
Advertising:	Trade publications, networking, memberships in real estate and general business organizations, referrals
Qualifications:	Real estate experience, close knowledge of your area's neighborhoods, attractions, amenities, schools
Equipment needed:	Office furniture, computer, printer, fax, modem, business card, letterhead, envelopes
Staff required:	No
Handicapped opportunity:	No
Hidden costs:	Telephone bills, membership dues, entertainment

Lowdown:

Your ideal market will probably be companies that do some relocations but are too small to provide much assistance in-house to the executives they are transferring to your community. Moving is a challenging experience for almost all families, and enlightened employers will see the value of your assistance in making the transition go as smoothly as possible. You will provide advice as the transferees begin to make decisions: What neighborhood will we like best? Where can we find eldercare or child care? What sports are played at local high schools? Can we find a house with enough land for trail riding? Your relocation consulting service will assist transferees with questions like these. You work with the employees before they are ready to choose a real estate agent.

Start-up:

Equipping your office will be the main expense (about $3,000). You will do some work by computer and fax, but most of your time will probably be spent driving to the different areas of your city, or having a restaurant meal with a transferee. Annual wages of $15,000 are realistic for part-time work.

Bottom Line Advice:

You're doing two kinds of marketing here, first, for your own service, and second, for your community. Many organizations use relocation consultants to help persuade a prospective employee to take the job with that company. How the prospect and his or her family feel about moving to your area can be a major factor. Your services can offer an unprejudiced look at what the locality has to offer. Hospitals recruiting a certain physician and companies recruiting someone for an upper-management position will both value your service highly.

Reminder Service

Start-up cost:	Under $1,000 ($500 to cover flyers and advertising); add $1,500 if you buy a computer
Potential earnings:	$10,000-$15,000
Typical fees:	$20-$35 per month
Advertising:	Bulletin boards, direct mail, networking at business meetings
Qualifications:	Strong organizational and time-management skills
Equipment needed:	Computer and software program with built-in reminders, a detailed planner
Staff required:	No (although you may want someone to cover the late shift)
Handicapped opportunity:	Yes
Hidden costs:	Telephone costs may be high if you're not careful; also, be sure to keep accurate records for billing purposes

Lowdown:

If you consider yourself exceptionally well-organized and have the ability to stay on top of a million details at once, then setting up a reminder service should come naturally to you. Your days will consist of talking with clients to determine the scope of their needs, entering their data onto a computerized tracking system, and keeping on top of what you need to remind them of and when. Set regular hours to maintain continuity; this cannot be a job that you work at only when you feel like it. Also, since many of your customers are too busy to remember important details of their lives (such as when to pay bills, birth dates of family and friends, and other such data), they may forget to pay you. That's why it is suggested that you collect at least half of your fee up front, offering standard hourly rates and/or specific packages geared toward themes. For instance, you could offer a "Birthday Blitz" package, where the only service the customer buys from you is that of being reminded of important birthdays as they occur throughout the year.

Start-up:

There are quite a few good time-management and reminder-type software packages out there, so do yourself a favor and buy the best one you can afford. You'll also need a powerful computer (about $1,500). After you get your computer system plugged in, all you really need are your marketing materials (flyers and business cards).

Bottom Line Advice:

Helping others to keep track of the important details of their lives, both personally and professionally, can be interesting and different work nearly every day. The downside is pretty clear-cut, however: mess up once, and your business could get a bad reputation. That's why you should protect yourself with a good software program to help manage your business.

Resume Service

Start-up cost:	$1,000-$5,000
Potential earnings:	$20,000-$50,000
Typical fees:	$150-$500 per resume (depending on your demographics)
Advertising:	Yellow Pages, newspaper classifieds, referrals
Qualifications:	Writing ability, attention to important detail, strong organizational ability
Equipment needed:	Computer, printer, fax/modem, paper, extra computer disks
Staff required:	No
Handicapped opportunity:	Yes
Hidden costs:	Insurance, spending too much time with one client

Lowdown:

Thousands of people are looking for new work these days, and they all have one need in common: they simply must have a dynamic resume. Those who really want to put their best foot forward with a trend-setting (yet somewhat traditional-looking) resume and cover letter will come to you for a package that looks visually appealing yet businesslike enough to get even a stuffed-shirt hiring professional to glance twice. Your resume service needs to reflect the trends of the future in order to survive, because the small typing service-variety resume service simply can't keep up with technological demands and self-promotional waves of the future. Some folks are even posting their resumes on the Internet, and you could offer additional services such as this if you choose. Regardless, your days will be spent meeting with a wide variety of clients from all walks of life (from foundry supervisors to attorneys), writing down specific job histories, and adding pertinent skill information that will make a potential employer jump with glee. It's a time-consuming job, but it gets easier the more you work at it.

Start-up:

Your start-up is relatively low ($1,000-$5,000) because all you really need is a good computer setup and a small advertising budget to get the word out. You can expect to earn $20,000 or so in most medium-size markets; in New York City and other large metropolitan areas, you'll be charging much more for your services (up to $500) and could easily make $50,000 per year.

Bottom Line Advice:

If you're a writer, this is a pretty easy way to make a living (or an additional income to support your quest for the Great American Novel). However, you do need to enjoy working with people: they will hound you day and night until their project is finished, and possibly even afterward. If you don't like to be hounded, stick to novel writing.

Expert Advice

What sets your business apart from others like it?

Katina Z. Jones has a nontraditional resume service called Going Places Self-Promotions, Inc., in Akron, Ohio. She says that her business is unique because it breaks many of the traditional rules of resume writing. "We do resumes that are not only eye-catching, but also go beyond providing a mere rundown of a client's job history. We like to add a sense of not only what a person has accomplished in their career, but also who they are and how they might fit into an organization. We have a 98 percent success rate in helping clients secure interviews because of that personalized approach."

Things you couldn't do without:

"I couldn't do without my computer, laser printer, phone, pager, and fax. My clients want fairly quick turnaround, and these items help me to accomplish that. Also, I need to have plenty of paper catalogs on hand, as I use a ton of specialty preprinted stationery to produce resumes on."

Marketing tips/advice:

"Set yourself apart from the people who are glorified typists . . . recognize that the resume industry is changing rapidly, and the resumes of the past (with cookie-cutter objectives and meaningless buzzwords) are just not getting people results anymore. After you've got your niche, network like crazy. Anywhere you go, introduce yourself; you're bound to meet someone who either needs a resume or knows someone who does."

If you had to do it all over again . . .

"I would have started networking much sooner and would also have put together a more meaningful marketing plan; I don't think I strategized nearly enough in the beginning."

Reunion Organizer

Start-up cost:	$2,000-$3,000
Potential earnings:	$15,000-$50,000
Typical fees:	$5-$10 for each classmate who attends
Advertising:	Word of mouth and warm calling
Qualifications:	A big network of friends and acquaintances in your community, patience, determination, organizational ability
Equipment needed:	Computer, database and suite software, fax, copier, office furniture, business card, letterhead, envelopes
Staff required:	No
Handicapped opportunity:	Yes
Hidden costs:	Telephone bills

Lowdown:

Changing life patterns are making reunions seem more appealing to many kinds of groups; more women in the workforce leaves fewer people with the time to pull such events together. High school reunions are a major focus of this business and finding the "lost" members is an important part of the process. Your persistence and sheer determination need to be applied to the search process, which usually starts one year before the event. Former employees of some organizations also occasionally hold reunions, and there is a niche market in putting together reunions for today's far-flung families. Once you discover the whereabouts of the people, you may turn your attention to the event itself, arranging the catering, photos, band, decorations, and mementos.

Start-up:

Basic office equipment ($2,000-$3,000) should get you started, but you will need to get the database program ($175-$300) as soon as possible. Set your charges differently for the time involved and the number of people you're expected to locate; many charge between $5-$10 per attendee, but others charge a flat rate commensurate with an hourly fee of $10-$15 per hour.

Bottom Line Advice:

Most communities are excellent markets for this service, but they don't know it yet. Reunion organizing is an obvious service to offer, but people won't be expecting it to be available. Consider the organizations and groups in your locale that have reunions, such as schools and colleges. Get a foothold, do one excellent job, and you will find that the referrals will begin to roll in. Your success will depend to some extent on the material and information you have to work with, but once you refine your people-searching skills, you should have a service to offer that can't be matched by amateurs. One tip: Use on-line phone books or the new telephone directories on disk or CD-ROM; these can help you locate nearly anyone in the country.

Roommate Referral Service

Start-up cost:	$500-$1,000
Potential earnings:	$10,000-$25,000
Typical fees:	20 to 50 percent of a month's rent
Advertising:	Yellow Pages, flyers at apartment complexes, coin-operated laundries, and supermarkets, newspaper classified ads
Qualifications:	Excellent organization skills
Equipment needed:	Database management software, computer modem, printer, phone, credit card processing equipment
Staff required:	No
Handicapped opportunity:	Yes
Hidden costs:	Insurance

Lowdown:

With the rising cost of living in many major cities, and the rise in displaced folks who need to share rent with the ideal roommate, you could make a fine living playing matchmaker for live-ins. Ideally, you would have a method for screening each of the candidates (police checks at the very least) and a method for securing your payment ahead of time (credit card processing equipment would be helpful). Advertise in places where people generally look for a place to live, and you'll have found your special niche. Develop a good questionnaire that really asks the kinds of questions a potential roommate would want answered. To double your income potential, you could add on other services such as mediation between rumblin' roomies or budget development assistance. The best advice is to focus on one area first, then branch out your services as you move successfully along.

Start-up:

Your costs are incredibly low when compared to most other businesses, mainly because you can create your own flyers to post in noticeable, highly trafficked areas. That's why your income potential, while seemingly low, is actually somewhat appealing—you have such low overhead, most of your income ($10,000-$25,000) will be sheer profit.

Bottom Line Advice:

The only advice is to be sure you carefully screen your applicants—bad matches are sure to strike you if you don't.

Keeping the Records You Need

Probably the most important device for managing the paperwork of your business is the circular file. Do not keep any piece of paper unless you are sure that you want it, or need it. Hanging a "Bless This Mess" sign over your desk is no solution. Instead, plan how you will manage your paper and just do it. You want to spend your time on profit-making tasks, not on searching through mountains of unorganized material for that one vital receipt or order slip.

What records are you required to keep? The IRS has issued certain guidelines: "Your permanent books (including inventory records) must show not only your gross income, but also your deductions and credits. In addition, you must keep any other records and data necessary to support the entries in your books and on your tax and information returns." This information includes paid bills and canceled checks. The IRS lets you decide how to store this material, as long as you choose an "orderly" approach.

For very small businesses, the checkbook register can be enough of a financial record, with one shoe box for receipts and another for invoices. Most organizations move rapidly past this stage, though. Spend a small amount of time planning for storage, and prevent yourself from wasting hours and hours at year-end as you prepare your figures for your accountant. Set up a filing system you feel comfortable with, and stick to it during the year. Color-coded file folders in hanging files are appropriate for almost all types of organizations.

There's nothing glamorous about file folders in a box, but this kind of system can expand as you grow. It lets you put your hand quickly on the paper you need and efficiently store the records you must keep. It gets stuff off your desk when you're not working on it, and it lets you have it back when you need it.

A popular approach is to devote one color to each major business topic. Marketing, for example, could be blue. You'd set up a tabbed hanging folder, in blue, for whatever marketing papers you have now. Later, you will probably need to subdivide the hanging folder with different tabbed blue file folders for your plan, your market research, new ideas, special promotion plans, sales forecasts, and so on. And remember that labeling the file folders is just as important as labeling those computer disks you probably have sliding around on your desk.

Further refinements to the filing system depend on the nature of your business. For salespeople, a tickler file system arranged by date may be essential: two weeks from now, which accounts should be called on? What should be done six months from now? For services, you may need files of information and concept-oriented material arranged by topic area: employee motivation, training systems, new approaches, etc.

Most businesses keep client files alphabetically. Your clients or customers are the lifeblood of your business, and you need a quick, efficient way of storing and retrieving their information: desires, wants, needs, buying history, future possibilities. The IRS may not care about this aspect of your business, but it's the basis of the ongoing marketing relationship that supports everything you do.

So choose a system, put it together, and put away every piece of paper you have kicking around your company. Keep using the files all year. Then you can stop thinking about this boring topic and get busy with the action steps that lead you toward your business goals.

Rubber Stamp Business

Start-up cost:	$5,000-$10,000
Potential earnings:	$40,000-$60,000
Typical fees:	Anywhere from $5-$15 per stamp
Advertising:	Mail order, direct mail, newspapers
Qualifications:	None (you can be trained by a printing professional)
Equipment needed:	Computer with laser printer, photopolymer system (you can subcontract the larger orders that need to be made of rubber)
Staff required:	No
Handicapped opportunity:	Yes
Hidden costs:	Materials can run high (as much as $1,000 per year)

Lowdown:

The rubber stamp business gets the stamp of approval from many entrepreneurial resources. Why? Because it's a relatively easy way to make steady money from a simple product. The variety of stamps you can produce is mind-boggling; think of the last time you went into a retail store and saw literally hundreds of choices (from frogs to stars to computers). Now think of the possibilities in the business world: small businesses need to have return address stamps; they're cheaper in the long haul than labels and more readily available as well. You can sell wholesale, retail, or mail order with this business, and expect to generate immediate interest if you introduce your company with introductory specials and discounts for new customers. You'll work with printers and graphics people who can provide you with all the background and technical information you need . . . so what's to lose from a product line so easy to produce?

Start-up:

You'll need to invest in some equipment ($3,000-$5,000) at the outset. If you're buying a franchise version of this business (which could provide you with all the training you'll need), expect to spend another $10,000 minimum on licensing fees. But, since you'll be marketing your inexpensive ($3-$15 each) product to the masses, you stand a good chance of making a go of this one.

Bottom Line Advice:

The investment's not too high, the income potential is high . . . what more could you ask?

Sales of Novelty and Promotional Products

Start-up cost:	$1,000-$5,000
Potential earnings:	$30,000-$60,000
Typical fees:	Each product sells anywhere from a few dollars to several hundred
Advertising:	Trade publications, business periodicals, direct mail, catalogs
Qualifications:	Sales ability
Equipment needed:	Computer, suite software, modem, fax, laser printer, business card, letterhead, envelopes, marketing materials
Staff required:	Probably
Handicapped opportunity:	Yes
Hidden costs:	Inventory, reprinting of catalogs and other sales materials

Lowdown:

This is the business for you if you know what will amuse people (namely, your clients' customers) and catch their attention. You are providing one facet of the activity that is essential to every business: marketing. Novelties and promotional materials put the name and message of a business out before the public. They can be an enormously effective way of reaching out for customers. In this process, you are far more than just a writer of orders. You present ideas for the new and different. Promotional materials can take many forms, and fitting the object to the message takes a special kind of business insight. You'll need to have an enthusiasm for sales and marketing in your blood. You need to be as creative and off-beat as possible to attract the attention of companies who want to attract attention to themselves.

Start-up:

Your relationship with your distributor will control your need for inventory, which ideally will be kept to a minimum. Demonstration samples and catalogs may be quite expensive, though. Try to secure a good arrangement with your manufacturers and their reps before trying to produce your own. You can earn a living selling these types of products; just look at how well companies such as Successories are doing and you'll know that the market is profitable.

Bottom Line Advice:

Your devotion to the needs of your clients will make you stand out from the crowd. There is quite a lot of competition in this field, but many of the other businesses just throw a catalog at prospects and expect them to do the creative work. You, on the other hand, develop a presentation focused on each client's distinctive needs and expectations. You give them several appealing options, and you carry out the detailed ordering and delivery process. It is work, but it's also fun.

Expert Advice

What sets your business apart from others like it?
"We have not only created a specialty product, but something that has a life and character all its own," says Mark Juarez, President and CEO of Tender Loving Things, Inc., in Oakland, California, which produces tiny wooden creatures with massage capability.

Things you couldn't do without:
"Birch or maple wood, drilling machine, glue, smiley-face brander and office equipment to run shipping, production, art, marketing, customer service, and administrative departments."

Marketing tips/advice:
"We turn profits into social responsibility; we donate 10 percent of our product to non-profit organizations and other groups that might benefit from the caring touch."

If you had to do it all over again . . .
"One of our biggest external challenges has been combating knockoffs and copycats." Juarez suggests protecting yourself as early as possible within federal trademark regulations.

Dynamic Goal-Setting

If you want to succeed in business, you need to start with a good goal-setting program. Seek out professional help in this area if you are not sure how to identify and set your own goals. Here are just a few tips to get you started:

1. Remember to make your goals specific. The only goals that stand a chance of being achieved are the ones that are clear enough to become part of a mind-set and visualization process. The clearer the goal, the easier to accomplish.
2. Have a deadline for achievement. You can have a terrific goal, but wander around aimlessly without a drop-dead date for its achievement. Someone once said that a goal is a dream with a deadline.
3. Consider and anticipate your obstacles. Know where the pitfalls might occur, and devise a plan to work around such impediments.

Above all else, make sure there is a personal benefit to achieving the goal, or it will not serve to motivate you. You need to reward yourself with a vacation if you sell one million dollars' worth of product, or you might not be able to see the benefit of working so hard to achieve that goal.

Scanning Service

Start-up cost:	$600-$1,000
Potential earnings:	$15,000-$25,000
Typical fees:	About $3 per page or image
Advertising:	Yellow Pages, local business newspapers
Qualifications:	Ability to use the software and scanner
Equipment needed:	Scanner, computer, optical character recognition and image scanning software
Staff required:	No
Handicapped opportunity:	Yes
Hidden costs:	Software upgrades

Lowdown:

Anyone who deals with document production beyond simple word processing will probably be needing a scanner anyway. So why not make some additional money with it by scanning for others? Paper records are scanned for businesses so that data can be stored, indexed, and accessed electronically. But many organizations that need this process do not own scanners and will bring their paperwork to you. Your other main market will be scanning images. Pasteup is going the way of the carrier pigeons. Everything must be part of the electronic file nowadays. You can scan images and store them as .TIF files for manipulation later by graphics designers, artists, and document production specialists.

Start-up:

Adding the scanner to your current office setup will not be excessively costly ($600-$1,000), especially in view of the fee you can charge for its use ($3 per image average). Be sure to buy a high-resolution scanner; save yourself a lot of aggravation by not purchasing a hand-held model (even though they are less expensive). For a scanning business, you'll need to produce your results quickly and accurately—and a hand-held model doesn't produce quality results.

Bottom Line Advice:

You're not going to build a business empire out of scanning alone, but it will likely round out other services you already offer. Marketing will bring some people to your door for scanning services alone, but you are most likely to be selling scanning to people you already work with.

Seamstress/Alterations Business

Start-up cost:	$1,000-$5,000 (depending on whether you have to rent space)
Potential earnings:	$20,000-$40,000
Typical fees:	Varied, but charges normally start at $5 and go all the way to $75, depending on what needs to be done
Advertising:	Newspapers, bulletin boards, fashion shows
Qualifications:	The ability to create fashions and apparel without patterns would be useful
Equipment needed:	Sewing machine and materials
Staff required:	No
Handicapped opportunity:	Possibly
Hidden costs:	Remakes could take up a lot of your time; make sure your work meets even the toughest standards

Lowdown:

If all you need is a needle and thread to design a business you feel comfortable in, then the alterations/sewing business is a perfect match. In this recession-proof business, you will repair or alter clothing that belongs to your client—but you can also offer custom-sewn clothing to busy executives who appreciate fine threads designed expressly for them. Creativity and the desire to make good clothes even better are the only requirements you'll need, and the higher the quality of your work, the more people will hear about your service. Word of mouth is nearly always the best way to grow the alterations business, although you may want to consider posting your business card on all the bulletin boards you can find in your community. Also, leave some extra cards for owners of dress shops—they often refer their customers to good tailors or seamstresses.

Start-up:

Your biggest up-front cost will be a good sewing machine (up to $1,000 or more); you might look into buying a used commercial sewing machine, because they are more durable and can be purchased for as little as $400. Be sure to invest in professional-looking business cards, because you'll need a lot of them to spread the word about your service. Use a rate card to keep track of what you're charging per job; some alterations are simple and inexpensive ($5-$10), while others are time-intensive and require you to charge $75 or more.

Bottom Line Advice:

If you like to work sparingly with people and spend much of the time by yourself, you'll love this type of work. However, the hours can be long and the rewards not as frequent as you might like. Sewing is tedious work except to those who truly enjoy it— so make sure that you enjoy it enough to spend 65 percent of your workday doing it.

Marketing Trends of the Future

How your business will look in the future depends upon your changing consumer base. Here are just a few trends:

- **The Age Factor.** The number of Americans over 65 exceeds the total population of Canada. Aging bodies have distinct needs in everything from health care to cosmetics. Aging minds may be in search of nostalgia as well as retirement planning.
- **Alternative Lifestyles.** Notice this in health issues (aromatherapy, organic foods, wellness programs) and in the move to the home office, to a slower pace of life, to spiritual fulfillment.
- **Cocooning.** People are claiming control of their immediate environments. This shows itself in increasing gun-ownership (particularly among women), in the rise in home-schooling, in people's reluctance to go to a business. You may have to go to your customers.
- **Adventure.** People want excitement, but they want it safely. The trend is toward exotic foods, sports, and travel.
- **The Informed Consumer.** Access to information allows a consumer to research your product before speaking to you. Be ready to listen, to get to know your customer, to establish trust.

These are some of the broad trends. Get to know the narrower trends, too, in your neighborhood and business area.

Secretarial Service

Start-up cost:	$3,000-$5,000
Potential earnings:	$20,000-$40,000
Typical fees:	$10-$20 per hour (depending on size of the company you're working for)
Advertising:	Classified ads, Yellow Pages, phone contacts
Qualifications:	Good typing and clerical skills
Equipment needed:	Computer or word processor, paper
Staff required:	No
Handicapped opportunity:	Yes
Hidden costs:	Invest in a freelance proofreader or proofreading software, as mistakes could cost you repeat business

Lowdown:

The executive stretches in his chair, puts his feet up on his desk, and calls for his secretary . . . only, in the age of downsizing, he's likely to be kept waiting—because she's sharing with ten others who are already in line with their requests. The old days where everyone had a personal secretary are gone; many functions have been replaced by small secretarial pools or computers. But the need for personalized service has not gone away, and often a beleaguered company, its small administrative force stretched to the max, needs to farm out work. That's where you come in. You can assist them for a short period of time, typing letters or producing manuals that would be simply too costly to employ a full-timer with benefits to do. Training and/or experience as a secretary will help you understand the types of skills that you need and an idea of who to offer them to (dictation, shorthand, filing, and form typing are just a few). There is a lot of flexibility possible with this type of business: after-regular-hours work for out-of-towners to temporary fill-ins for local companies to contracting overflow and everything in between.

Start-up:

A computer is the recommended choice for running a secretarial service since it has greater versatility and a variety of available programs (compatible, of course, with your client's), but a word processor could work in a beginning pinch. Computers will cost anywhere from $1,000-$3,000, while a simple word processor can be bought for as low as $500. Whichever you choose, buying used models only a year or two old will help keep start-up costs down. Advertising in the Yellow Pages for $50-$100 per month, in the classifieds for $10 per week, and leaving flyers at hotels where businesspeople from out-of-town might need some help are some easy, inexpensive ways to get word out about the services being offered. Remember, the amount of time it will take to finish one assignment will vary and is generally unknown at the start, so charging an hourly fee of $10-$15 will prove more profitable than working for a set price per task.

Bottom Line Advice:

Since it's likely that this job will involve working with many different people, tolerance of personality quirks will make jobs—and time—go more quickly and smoothly. The hours will be varied, which could become stressful for you (and your bank account) at times. This business needs a high-energy, go-getter type of person; do you have what it takes (and can you take the orders placed upon you by others)?

Expert Advice

What sets your business apart from others like it?

"I'm incredibly fast, accurate, and affordable," says Jana McClish, owner of Paragon Word Services in Akron, Ohio. "I can offer a quicker turnaround than most of my competitors."

Things you couldn't do without:

McClish needs a computer, answering machine, and a calculator to run her business effectively.

Marketing tips/advice:

"You have to be persistent and market almost constantly. You must be confident and be able to sell that confidence in order to get in the door. You really need to have a special skill that sets you apart, too."

If you had to do it all over again . . .

"I'd research my equipment purchases better. I needed to buy new equipment a year and a half into my business because I did not purchase wisely. Also, I would've started with a much bigger base of prospects . . . I got kind of discouraged in the beginning because I didn't have huge amounts of work."

Silk Flower Arranger

Start-up cost:	$500-$1,000
Potential earnings:	$20,000-$40,000
Typical fees:	$25-$300
Advertising:	Yellow Pages, newspapers, bridal salons, restaurants
Qualifications:	Some training with flower arranging, creativity
Equipment needed:	Phone, floral accessories (vases, baskets, floral tape, access to a wide variety of silk flowers)
Staff required:	No
Handicapped opportunity:	Yes
Hidden costs:	Watch materials costs

Lowdown:

There's nothing in the world like fresh flowers, but they only last a short while. That's why silk flowers are the mainstays of interior decorating; all you've got to do is dust them every once in a while and they retain their beauty forever. You'll always have plenty of customers if you choose to work in this field, from brides who don't want to worry about wilting flowers, to mourners who want to give the bereaved family a lasting token of their remembrance. You'll work many hours in your office, putting together the arrangements that have been ordered by your customers. The only problem is, you'll have to work hard to get some business, since there are plenty of others like you. Think about what makes you different, and let your customers know exactly what your unique marketing point is. Finally, network with funeral homes, churches, and wedding shops for cross-marketing opportunities.

Start-up:

Obtain a vendor's license (approximately $25) and buy your supplies at a wholesale store. Check with local craft stores to see if they offer additional discounts if you have a vendor's license. When starting the business, invest a few hundred dollars in floral supplies and silk flowers so you can make arrangements to sell at craft shows. Also, set aside money for booth space rental ($25-$100). Your products will sell anywhere from $25-$300.

Bottom Line Advice:

Gain experience by working with florists or taking classes at craft stores. Once you have some knowledge of floral arranging, sign up to sell your goods at holiday craft fairs. Always have plenty of business cards/brochures to accompany each sale, and keep an album with pictures of your work to show clients.

Stenciling

Start-up cost:	$1,000-$2,000
Potential earnings:	$1,000-$3,000 per month
Typical fees:	$25-$1,000 per project
Advertising:	Business cards, bulletin boards, craft stores, specialty clothing shops, paint and wallpaper stores
Qualifications:	Some artistic flare, ability to handle repetitious work
Equipment needed:	Various paint brushes, sponges, stenciling patterns, paint and varnishes
Staff required:	No
Handicapped opportunity:	Yes
Hidden costs:	Insurance

Lowdown:

This is a centuries-old technique believed to have started in the Fiji Islands. Even today, folks like having their walls and homes decorated, so you should have no problem getting business. There are as many techniques of stenciling as there are surfaces to stencil. Many people are afraid to stencil their own walls, so they'll hire a professional like you to come in and do the work (which can actually be quite fun once you know what you're doing). You can also stencil floors, furniture, and all types of fabrics. If you want to get into home interior stenciling, hook up with custom builders who provide referrals or contract the work out themselves. Take along some pictures of other stenciling you've done in your own home. If you want to hit the craft shows, the sky's the limit on what you can stencil on—and what you can sell. At shows, the more unique the item, the better it sells.

Start-up:

Stenciling is relatively inexpensive to start ($1,000-$2,000). Your hidden cost may come in the form of a bolt of cloth or a bench to stencil on (about $300 to start). Also, if you do the craft shows, know that you'll have to pay for table or floor space (typically $150-$400 a pop). Most nonprofessional stencilers do this as a hobby; others make $1,000-$3,000 per month, depending on how many jobs they can get.

Bottom Line Advice:

Stenciling can be done on everything, from food to kites to cars. If you don't see a stencil out there you like, you can make your own with minimal effort. If you don't want to pay for a stencil pattern, your local library is full of them. Stenciling may require long periods of standing or sitting. You might want to work in a ventilated area because of fumes from the paint and varnishes.

Stenography Service

Start-up cost:	$3,000-$6,000
Potential earnings:	$30,000-$40,000
Typical fees:	$15 per page, or $20 per hour
Advertising:	Newspapers, Yellow Pages, publications targeting the business community, referrals
Qualifications:	Secretarial skills, good organizational ability
Equipment needed:	Word-processing equipment, dictation machine, excellent printer, fax
Staff required:	No
Handicapped opportunity:	Yes
Hidden costs:	Software upgrades, office supplies

Lowdown:

Stenography is a service that can be marketed widely to businesses that are under-staffed or have very lean organizational structures. Your ability to get dictation transcribed accurately onto paper, on time, can be a valuable addition to your clients' work processes. Senior managers have assumed that the advent of the computer has removed the need for stenographic services. They're no longer available in many corporations, but the need is definitely still there, and you can fill it. With the growth of small business establishments in most areas, you could find another market in the very small enterprises that have no support staff at all.

Start-up:

Your furniture must allow you to work comfortably. You'll need equipment compatible with that of your clientele ($3,000 to start). You could earn upward of $40,000.

Bottom Line Advice:

Depending on your locality you may find quite a bit of competition for the services you offer. Pricing your work so that you can meet the competition and make an appropriate profit may be a challenge. It may take you a while to learn to give accurate estimates and set appropriate prices. You'll also need to be a self-starter, able to keep going without the stimulation of a busy workplace to keep you on task. Of course, some people find it easier to get work done without the hubbub of the social scene that's usual in a large organization.

Storyteller

Start-up cost:	$100-$500
Potential earnings:	$5,000-$15,000
Typical fees:	$15-$25 per storytelling event
Advertising:	Boards of Education, day care centers, libraries
Qualifications:	Ability to tell and retell stories with enthusiasm
Equipment needed:	None (except a great archive of stories)
Staff required:	No
Handicapped opportunity:	Yes
Hidden costs:	Books

Lowdown:

Do you have a flair for telling (and retelling) stories? Can you paint pictures in listeners' minds as they hear every exciting detail? You may be skilled in the ancient art of story-telling; it's a tradition that first reached popularity during the time of Homer's *The Odyssey*. Now, storytellers for children are especially popular; many schools regularly bring in such professionals and parents are increasingly seeking storytellers for parties and special events. But storytelling isn't just reading well from a book; it's memorizing the stories, adding your own personal touches where necessary, and enlivening stories in a way only you would choose to do. You'll need a good repertoire to choose from, and you'll have to practice regularly to ensure that your vocal abilities and versatility stay up to the job. More than likely, this will be a part-time business opportunity.

Start-up:

You'll have virtually no start-up cost except business cards or flyers and the books from which you'll glean your tantalizing tales. Spend about $100-$500 on these items and subscribe to magazines that contain storytelling tips or new stories. You won't get rich doing this (especially charging $15-$25 per event), but if you really love storytelling, the joy of sharing with children will be reward enough.

Bottom Line Advice:

Get involved with libraries in the area that feature children's activities. Place your business card in toy stores and bakeries, anywhere parents would go to plan for a child's birthday party.

Stress Management Counselor

Start-up cost:	$500-$1,500
Potential earnings:	$50,000-$65,000
Typical fees:	$20-$40 per session
Advertising:	Newspapers, magazines, bulletin boards, associations, physician referral, direct mail
Qualifications:	Some states require certification or license
Equipment needed:	Materials such as books, videos, audio tapes
Staff required:	No
Handicapped opportunity:	Yes
Hidden costs:	Certification can cost you anywhere from $200-$500, depending on your area. Also, corporate clients may have a 45-day payment delay policy, tying up your cash flow (so insist on at least 50 percent down)

Lowdown:

In the high-tech, fast-food '90s, we are all getting stressed out to the max—and that's why stress management counselors have been cropping up everywhere, from church groups to Corporate America. Large companies hire such professionals to keep their employees sound, sane, and productive—recognizing that a well-balanced worker is also as much as 45 percent more effective on the job. As a stress management counselor, you would work with individuals or groups, assessing their problem areas and assisting them through innovative, inspiring materials and exercises. You will encourage them to perform at their happiest and healthiest best.

Start-up:

To begin with, you'll need to promote your services to literally hundreds of people; however, you should pinpoint the top 50 or so prospects and exhaust your efforts there before embarking on the rest of the world. Buy or develop a list of human resource professionals to mail information to—and don't forget to secure a vendor's license if you plan to offer resource materials for sale.

Bottom Line Advice:

You'll feed off of the creative energy generated by helping others solve stress problems; after all, it is much easier for an outsider to identify what's working and what's not. After a few years, though, you may burn out yourself . . . make sure you've got a support person who will remind you of that which you preach.

Taste Tester for Food Companies

Start-up cost:	$500
Potential earnings:	$10,000-$15,000 (most work part-time hours)
Typical fees:	$10-$15 per hour
Advertising:	Direct mail to food product manufacturers
Qualifications:	A good culinary sense and strong tastebuds
Equipment needed:	None
Staff required:	No
Handicapped opportunity:	Yes
Hidden costs:	Mileage can become a problem; see that you are reimbursed or that you've covered these costs in your pricing structure

Lowdown:

The ultimate dream job for those who love food! Companies that are producing food products often use outside individuals for taste testers; although it is not a particularly lucrative field, it can be an interesting and satisfying one filled with variety. As a taste tester, you will taste new or improved food products and record your impressions, usually on a checklist predesigned by the company. You may have to wear a blindfold for some tests, while others may simply require a thumbs-up or thumbs-down. It is important that you can communicate to others the palatability of food; its taste, texture, and desirability are all of critical importance to the developers and marketing professionals working on the new product.

Start-up:

Buy a good list of companies that produce food items and you're off to a great start! With as little as an introductory letter detailing your interest in becoming a taste tester, you could let companies know of your availability—but do be sure to include some of your qualifications (such as having worked in a restaurant, or as a gourmet cook). You should have dependable transportation to and from company sites, because very rarely will you taste food in your own home.

Bottom Line Advice:

While working in a "food festival of the senses" can be easy to digest, it can also cause heartburn if you are seeking to build a large nest egg. Nowhere will you find a wealthy taste tester basking in just desserts. Still, if financial reward isn't as necessary or important to you, you could really eat your heart out with this small business opportunity. And the hours aren't all that bad, either.

Telemarketing Service

Start-up cost:	$6,000-$10,000
Potential earnings:	$40,000 or more
Typical fees:	$30 an hour
Advertising:	Yellow Pages, direct mail, business publications, membership in local business and civic groups
Qualifications:	Experience, persistence, ability to market your own service, writing skills for preparing script and reports
Equipment needed:	Telephone with headset, ergonomic office furniture, computer, suite software, printer, fax, modem, business card, letterhead, envelopes
Staff required:	No
Handicapped opportunity:	Yes
Hidden costs:	Utility bills, marketing time, and materials

Lowdown:

Telemarketing is a specialized and very focused form of marketing. No business can survive without effective marketing, and your challenge will be to reach the organizations that need to develop their customer base and show them how your service can help them grow. Telemarketing can be informational—a way of doing market research—but the major proportion will be focused on sales. As a small business, you may choose to offer a specific type of telemarketing: pharmaceuticals, commercial photography, wedding services, etc. This specialization will help you focus on your own marketing.

Start-up:

You'll need excellent telephone equipment and reasonably sophisticated computer equipment to track results and produce reports (about $6,000 to start). Once you get the hang of it, you can make $40,000 annually.

Bottom Line Advice:

People skills are even more important to success as a telemarketer than they are in other types of small businesses. Listening well, speaking convincingly, and tuning the message to the receiver are all essential. You'll need experience writing effective scripts, and you'll need patience and persistence. It will probably take some time to develop the client base for your business. You can distinguish yourself from the run-of-the-mill telemarketers because you're not someone just hired off the street. You have experience, you're creating a proven track record, and you have an unquenchable enthusiasm for your clients' projects.

Expert Advice

What sets your business apart from others like it?
"While there are many marketing and advertising agencies, public relations firms, and telemarketing organizations, my company is a one-stop agency that has the capability of coordinating any and all aspects of a marketing plan," says Cheryl D. Cira, owner of Columbus, Ohio-based Marketing Dimensions. "I cannot stress how important it is to be honest and up front with your customers. Marketing Dimensions looks at each project and account as a long-term relationship."

Things you couldn't do without:
"Essentials include telephone equipment and office furniture. It also helps to have computers in order to enter large lists, track calls, pull up records, and run reports. Computers are also used for simple design work, database management, and mail merges," says Cira.

Staffing tips/advice:
"Telemarketing projects depend on the work and devotion of employees. And, because people are people, there are some aspects that cannot be controlled, such as employees quitting without notice, coming in late, and calling in sick time after time. My office manager is very good at juggling schedules and maintaining a strong pool of telemarketers, but it can get crazy at times."

If you had to do it all over again . . .
"I don't think there is any one thing of great importance that I would change or do differently. In general, however, I wish that I had had more hands-on experience in managing a large staff and more working knowledge related to personnel issues."

Time-Management Specialist

Start-up cost:	$1,000-$6,500
Potential earnings:	$20,000-$40,000
Typical fees:	$75-$100 per hour or a set fee ($100+ per person) for classes you offer
Advertising:	Free workshops/seminars and other public speaking, word-of-mouth referrals, networking, news releases, written articles
Qualifications:	High level of organization, analytical ability, punctuality, ability to deliver on your commitments, an open mind
Equipment needed:	Computer with fax/modem, printer, phone, time-management software, handout materials
Staff required:	No
Handicapped opportunity:	Yes
Hidden costs:	Preparation time if you are not already using a previously written program, licensing fees if you are

Lowdown:

Bringing relief to people under inordinate stress is just one of the many benefits of being a time-management specialist. In addition to making the workplace a little less of a sweatshop, you'll be assisting clients in goal-setting, developing action plans, defining priorities, and scheduling/delegating tasks and activities. You may decide to work as a consultant, identifying problems for harried company executives in search of an answer in the pursuit of higher productivity. But you may also decide to add on additional services, such as seminars for large groups or individual personal productivity training. The opportunities to make money from time are there, you just need to send the message out to the people most in need of your services (and they are nowhere near as limited as you at first might think). Quick profitability is a definite possibility with this low overhead business—but you need to charge appropriately for your time and expertise. One last tip: Don't forget to offer periodic refresher courses for repeat business; you'd be surprised how many customers say they'd benefit from another session.

Start-up:

Word-of-mouth advertising keeps initial costs low in this business, because it is based on credibility and trust of the specialist. To present a professional image, allow a minimum of $250 for business cards, letterhead, and brochures. Computer costs can range from $1,500-$5,000. Remember that organizational dues will be necessary to continually network and prospect for clients; set aside at least $250 per year for this valuable lead-generator. Charge at least $75 per hour for corporate consulting; more ($1,000 per day is typical) if you're conducting seminars for groups of professionals.

Bottom Line Advice:

The art of timeliness and organization is relatively new to businesses. Hence, competition may not be a significant problem. If you enjoy leading others to dramatic results in a short period of time, this career can be extremely enjoyable. But you should be advised that this work demands a lot of your own time and energy to get started. Are you able to practice what you preach? It may take as much as a year or two before you are able to make a full-time income; hopefully, you have been gifted with patience yourself.

Expert Advice

What sets your business apart from others like it?

Jennifer Annandono, Managing Partner of the Kent, Ohio-based Progressive Leadership Center, says her business is unique because she is. "I greatly enjoy demonstrating to others how to have a more balanced work and personal life. My feeling is that time management is about setting goals, and the implementation of new tools, which will promote achievement."

Things you couldn't do without:

Annandono says she could not do without a second telephone line with answering or voice mail capability. "My computer and laser printer allow me the convenience of professional correspondence."

Marketing tips/advice:

"It is always more effective to market your service as the 'benefit' customers will receive rather than focusing on various features you might offer. Much of my marketing success is based in community interaction and word-of-mouth referral. The best advice is: always be a product of the service you provide!"

If you had to do it all over again . . .

"I would have spent the months preceding the opening of my business selecting centers of influence. If you are not already established in the community, it is never too early to identify and communicate with those individuals who know and trust you and clearly understand what service you provide."

Toy Cleaning Service

Start-up cost:	$500-$1,000
Potential earnings:	$20,000-$30,000
Typical fees:	$15-$20 per toy
Advertising:	Yellow Pages, direct mail, cold calls, referrals
Qualifications:	None (just elbow grease)
Equipment needed:	Standard germicidal spray/janitorial cleaning supplies, towels, gloves
Staff required:	No
Handicapped opportunity:	Yes
Hidden costs:	Excessive mileage (be sure to stay within a 40-mile radius unless you charge extra for work outside your territory)

Lowdown:

One innovative new business to hit the scene is a toy cleaning service for doctors' offices, playgrounds, restaurants, and child care centers that could use a helping hand keeping their toy collection clean and germ-free. All of these facilities leave hundreds of small toys in their waiting and play areas for children to use freely—often forgetting that each toy must be cleaned on a regular basis to avoid contamination among the children. You offer peace of mind to the folks who have the play center, while at the same time offering peace of mind to parents who worry about their children catching a cold or virus from dirty toys. And all you're doing is showing up, cleaning the toys properly, and returning everything neatly to its place. It's simple, it's straightforward—and the best part is, it's profitable because it's just one less chore for the customer to worry about.

Start-up:

All you really need is some germicidal spray and other cleaning solvents, gloves, and towels—everything under $500. Spend another $500 or so on advertising via direct mail or Yellow Pages (but keep in mind that until people know what you do, you're better off spending your advertising budget on direct mail and networking functions). If you build enough contacts, you could earn between $20,000-$30,000 per year—more if you grow and hire additional help.

Bottom Line Advice:

It's an innovative, yet totally sensible idea. All you need to do is get out there, convince others that you can save them time and money in the long run, and roll up your sleeves. It's a terrific little niche market for those who enjoy the cleaning business.

Travel Agent

Start-up cost:	$2,000-$5,000
Potential earnings:	$25,000-$45,000
Typical fees:	Commission of 10 percent is fairly common on each sale; some airlines have been cutting those commissions considerably, however
Advertising:	Travel, meeting/hotel magazines, Yellow Pages, direct mail, location
Qualifications:	Knowledge of the travel industry and particular destinations; often, certification is required through an accredited travel school; training on the customized computer systems most travel agencies use
Equipment needed:	At minimum, a computer and phone
Staff required:	No
Handicapped opportunity:	Yes
Hidden costs:	Phone expenses

Lowdown:

Would you find satisfaction helping others fly the friendly skies to exotic places? Have you always been a travel nut? If you answered yes to both questions, you could potentially succeed as a travel agent. As an outside travel agent, you would associate with a travel agency willing to work with you. You can refer business to them (for perhaps a 10 percent commission) or actually arrange travel bookings for which the agency will cut the tickets (because restrictions on ticketing won't allow you to do it). For the latter work, you can make as much as 60 to 70 percent of the commission. There are also networked travel agencies that rely almost solely on home-based agents, so your options are many if you decide to embark on this exciting and interesting business. The best part is, many travel companies offer incentives and special perks for agents like you—and you could wind up doing some sightseeing yourself.

Start-up:

You need a budget for advertising, the appropriate computer and office equipment, software, and phone, and may have to pay small fees (such as $50) to use your associate's name and ticketing number.

Bottom Line Advice:

The travel business is huge—and still growing by leaps and bounds. Many opportunities exist to make money in this field. The cost of running a travel business is modest if you are working as an outside agent; little more than computer and office equipment is required. Opening your own agency is an expensive proposition; it also takes time to get established, and competition from larger agencies capable of booking large corporate accounts can be daunting.

Expert Advice

Elizabeth C. Hatch
Travel Agent

On Improving Your Skills

I would definitely say: get experience. Don't open up an agency just because you are a person who likes to travel. When I started out, I was able to do everybody's job. I could be an account manager, I could take reservations, I could deliver tickets. I did everything.

If you're just a vacation agent, you're going to have to learn how to service corporate clients. If you're just a corporate agent, you're going to have to know how to do vacation sales. So get as much experience as you can in all of those different areas because you're going to need it when the opportunity arises.

On Personnel

When starting your own agency, or starting your own business in general, you need to be able to fill in for absent personnel in case of an emergency. When I first started and only had one other agent, if I was unable to work, I effectively lost 50 percent of my staff. You can't afford to be down to 50 percent of your staff when service is your product.

Being able to do everyone else's job also gains you greater respect from your employees. When they have a challenge or a question, I'm usually a good source for answers because I do understand what they are going through.

Expert Advice

What sets your business apart from others like it?

"My agents and I have traveled to almost every destination in the world, so I would say that personal experience sets us apart from other travel agents," says Helen Meek, owner of Helen Meek Travel in Fairlawn, Ohio.

Things you couldn't do without:

Computers with specialized reservation programs (leased from airline companies) and telephones are the primary pieces of equipment needed to run this travel agency. "We also couldn't do without our experienced, wonderful staff."

Marketing tips/advice:

"You need to look at location and market demographics; I knew my area would grow, and now I'm an established leader in my geographic location." Meek also advises entrepreneurs to get their names out there any way possible while building credibility.

If you had to do it all over again . . .

"Nothing. It's worked for thirteen years, and if you can get past those first five, you are probably going to make it."

Upholsterer

Start-up cost:	$1,000-$5,000
Potential earnings:	$20,000-$40,000
Typical fees:	Varied; could be as low as $50 and as high as $1,000
Advertising:	Yellow Pages, community newspapers, coupon books, referral
Qualifications:	Skilled apprenticeship
Equipment needed:	Upholstery tools, tacks, fabric
Staff required:	No
Handicapped opportunity:	Not typically
Hidden costs:	Insurance

Lowdown:

There's nothing like a terrific-looking accent chair to make any room stand out . . . and you can help your customers highlight any of their furniture pieces as a quality-driven upholsterer. If you've got the background or skill in the centuries-old art of upholstery, you could go into business as quickly as you can hang up a sign. All you need to do is make sure you're reaching the more affluent types; they'll generally pay better and have furniture re-covered more frequently. Once you've established yourself as a trusted name in the business, you'll be surprised how quickly referrals will start rolling in. Then you can spend your days helping customers choose new and exciting fabrics, style-enhancing accents (such as decorative tacks or tassels), and other details that will change the look and personality of each piece of furniture you work on. You'll provide an estimate, then set about the work itself (after you've ordered the requested fabric and materials). It's a challenging, creative business for those who truly love furniture.

Start-up:

You'll need $1,000-$5,000 to get started in this business, mainly to cover your equipment and supply costs. Of course, there will be at least $1,000 or so in advertising, too. However, if you are conscientious and pay attention to small details, your reputation could bring you $20,000-$40,000 per year.

Bottom Line Advice:

The work is exacting, physical—and, to some, quite tedious. If you prefer working alone in a quiet place, and if you are especially very task-oriented, this could be a wonderful opportunity for you. Remember, too, that there is plenty of room for creativity—and some furniture designers look to upholsterers for fresh ideas.

Vacation Rentals Broker

Start-up cost:	$500-$1,000
Potential earnings:	$45,000-$60,000
Typical fees:	Usually a percentage (10 to 15 percent)
Advertising:	Advertising in real estate magazines and real estate section of newspaper, Yellow Pages, referrals
Qualifications:	Experience in real estate rentals, good organizational skills
Equipment needed:	A basic office setup for record keeping
Staff required:	No
Handicapped opportunity:	No
Hidden costs:	Insurance, vehicle maintenance

Lowdown:

A vacation rentals broker keeps track of all the details related to renting property for distant owners. Many people with second homes rent them for the better part of the year, reserving a week or two for themselves and their families. Renting helps with the costs of this additional residence, but it also creates a number of headaches and problems that are very difficult for someone who lives far away to deal with. Your service finds renters, writes the rental contract, and makes sure that the agreements are carried out. You collect the rent, check for any damage, answer the million and one questions renters always have, and generally keep an eye on things.

Start-up:

Costs are minimal; you just need an effective way to keep track of information and money. Since your business depends directly on how much time you put into it, expect to earn as much as you work for (and that could be anywhere from $45,000-$60,000 or more).

Bottom Line Advice:

Consider becoming a vacation rentals broker if you live in an area that has a high appeal for renters and a large stock of available summer (or winter) homes to rent. Once you develop a reputation for dependability, referrals will bring other homeowners to you. The amount of advertising you will need to do will vary depending on your area and the presence or absence of competing services.

Wellness Instructor

Start-up cost:	$500-$1,500
Potential earnings:	$25,000-$40,000
Typical fees:	$20-$40 per hour
Advertising:	Human resource association newsletters, Yellow Pages
Qualifications:	Some states require certification
Equipment needed:	Fax, phone, pager or cellular phone
Staff required:	No
Handicapped opportunity:	Yes
Hidden costs:	Photocopying materials for classes can add up—be sure to include them in your price or cost analysis

Lowdown:

Rising medical costs have driven many companies to wellness programs as a preventive measure for cost containment. You can provide seminars for these companies on topics such as stress-cutting foods, the importance of drinking water throughout the day, and even breathing exercises. You'll rely on resource materials such as audiocassettes, books, and videos that give added credibility to what you teach. The fact is, most of us are leading potentially destructive lifestyles (drinking too much caffeine and smoking, for example) and need to be given some empowerment in our lives to conquer these bad habits. As a wellness instructor, your job will be to help clear out the cobwebs in mind, body, and spirit—and to do it in such a way that the students feel empowerment over their own bugaboos.

Start-up:

You can start a healthy business with a minimal investment if you have the right credentials (a degree in nursing, social work, or psychology). Advertising will initially cost you in the neighborhood of $500-$1,000, because you need to be where human resource and other professionals can readily find you (more specifically, in their trade association newsletter). One easy way to get your foot in the door is to attend professional functions and distribute your brochure or business card; most associations will allow nonmembers to attend meetings at a slightly higher cost than members. Take advantage—and promote the positive benefits of your work!

Bottom Line Advice:

Inspiring others to take charge of their lives and active roles in their health and longevity can be a richly rewarding field. But you'll need to make sure you follow your own rules; be a good role model and never, ever let them see you sweat!

Word-Processing Service

Start-up cost:	$5,000-$15,000
Potential earnings:	$30,000-$45,000
Typical fees:	Many in this field charge $5-$10 per page
Advertising:	Yellow Pages, focus advertising in a 5-10-mile radius of your business location, direct mail, university bulletin boards, networking with business and professional organizations
Qualifications:	Fast and accurate typing skills (at least 65 words per minute), customer-oriented attitude
Equipment needed:	Computer hardware and software, laser printer, modem, copy machine, fax; optional: transcribing machine and scanner.
Staff required:	None initially
Handicapped opportunity:	Yes
Hidden costs:	Equipment and software upgrades

Lowdown:

Despite the abundance of personal computers, demand for off-site word-processing services has steadily increased. Essentially, word-processing is a fancier (and more technically correct) phrase for typing service. You'll be doing all the same kinds of work, only you'll be using a computer instead of the great typewriter dinosaur. Customers will come to you with everything from reports and term papers to resumes and technical documentation. The ability to produce an attractive product with quick turnaround will ensure your success in this fairly competitive field. Remember that just about anybody with a basic computer system and printer thinks of getting into this type of business; you'll have to be able to set yourself apart from these folks as well as the hundreds of secretarial services out there (who perform services that go beyond your own). Position yourself close to a university or in a downtown area, and you'll increase your chances of success by at least 50 percent.

Start-up:

Your start-up costs are going to be quite reasonable if you already own a computer and laser printer. Most of your initial expense will result from advertising and appropriate software purchases (set aside at least $3,000 for these). Charge a per-page rate of $5-$10 or an hourly fee for the larger jobs; it'll take you a while to get a feel for which projects are more labor-intensive.

Bottom Line Advice:

Beware of underpricing your service. Consider adding a surcharge for handwritten or hard-to-read documents and materials that include charts or tables. If you can stand the repetitive motion of using a keyboard, and of typing other people's work, your income is limited only by your speed and the number of hours you want to work.

Workers' Compensation Consultant

Start-up cost:	$5,000-$7,000
Potential earnings:	$45,000-$60,000
Typical fees:	Monthly retainer fee of $1,500-$3,000 (depending on the size of the company)
Advertising:	Business periodicals, networking, referrals
Qualifications:	Ability to locate best rates for companies and ways to keep costs down
Equipment needed:	Computer, printer, office furniture, business card, letterhead, envelopes
Staff required:	No
Handicapped opportunity:	Yes
Hidden costs:	Insurance, membership dues

Lowdown:

A workers' compensation consultant is an outside contractor who works with companies to reduce the incidence of workers' compensation claims and to find better rates and innovative ways to save money. You will investigate the circumstances of the manner in which the employer deals with these problems. You might even administer the claims process for a period of time, instead of having a company employee do it. Typical strategies to reduce claims include: 1) more thoroughly investigating the claim to determine whether it is indeed valid; 2) conducting regular reviews of workers' compensation benefits packages; and 3) recommending changes in the workplace to reduce injuries. The bottom line is, your nose for trouble can prevent a company from being taken advantage of—either by invalid claims or high rates.

Start-up:

Investigative tools and the equipment to write reports are what you will need; spend at least $4,000 equipping your office with computer and printing equipment. Your reports will need to be clear and easy to understand (after all, they hired you to clear up the red tape, right?), so buy a decent software package for all of your major communications. Most disability consultants work on a retainer (typically $1,500-$3,000 per month).

Bottom Line Advice:

This is quite a lively field. To establish yourself you will probably need the experience gained from having been a workers' compensation specialist for an employer, or at least another consulting firm. If you show that you can conduct excellent investigations, write effective reports, and make productive recommendations for improvements in processes, you can build a very successful enterprise. You will not be everyone's favorite person as you uncover cheaters, but you will be improving your clients' bottom line.

Web Home Page Creator

Start-up cost:	$2,000-$3,000
Potential earnings:	$15,000+ (it's an emerging market, so the true ceiling isn't known yet)
Typical fees:	$500+ per creation
Advertising:	Word of mouth, bulletin board services, trade journals, on-line account
Qualifications:	Marketing skills, computer graphics and programming skills, experience in cyberspace
Equipment needed:	Computer, modem, office furniture
Staff required:	No
Handicapped opportunity:	Yes
Hidden costs:	Be sure to watch your connect time with on-line services

Lowdown:

This is about as cutting edge as you can get in the world of marketing. Industries of almost all types are exploring the Internet; many have found that a home page connects them with their customers in new ways. An effective full-color home page works much better than a dull list of products available with their specs. Producing an effective home page is an entirely different experience from developing an old-fashioned paper brochure; if you can make the Web come alive for a client by designing a home page that is visited often, you can be one of the first in this emerging field. Businesses need to understand that surfers will spend time at a location on the Internet that offers something they want: an interesting, informative home page that engages their imaginations and offers them products related to their needs.

Start-up:

Power up your modem and go. On-line time will probably be a significant cost and you will want to advertise on-line as well; these rates will vary according to carrier but run $20 a month for basic services and an average of $4 per hour on extended services. Set your fees according to what the market will bear—check out what competitors are charging by visiting their Internet site.

Bottom Line Advice:

This business depends on several kinds of creativity at once. The process of making home pages isn't something you can follow step-by-step out of your old college textbooks. You're covering new ground here. It will take creativity to market yourself as well, because the whole idea of computerized marketing is so new. Learning about your client companies so you can represent them creatively and effectively will keep you on your mental toes. You'll find it takes quite a bit of time to find clients creative and futuristic enough to understand the advantages of your service.

Expert Advice

Jeff Chin and Time Regan
Web Home Page Creators

On Having a Business Plan

When we first started our business together, we said, "We don't need a business plan. We know what we're doing. We know where we're going with this, and the business plan might actually inhibit our opportunities." We were so wrong! No matter what your business is, develop a plan, and structure that plan with some realistic objectives and benchmarks, and stick with it. And once you get to a point where you've allowed yourself the room to shift a little bit, then do it. But a business plan is absolutely critical. We missed perhaps six or eight months of business opportunities because we didn't have a plan.

To sustain your business for any length of time, you're going to need to invest money as well as time. When you're first starting out, you should have some money from your last job in reserve for basic expenses. Even if you're starting your business on the side, you're going to have to spend money on marketing and hardware. The more you have tucked away, the more comfortable you will be.

If we could start our business over again, we would put more money into marketing up front. We spent a lot of money on equipment, software, and education. The learning process was long and expensive. In retrospect, we should have approached smaller potential clients and offered to handle assignments while we were still going through the learning process. It probably would have been easier too, if we had two or three more people on board.

Part III

Appendix

Listing of Businesses by Category

Arts & Crafts

Candle Maker
Caning Specialist
Collectibles/Memorabilia
Doll Repair Service
Jewelry Designer
Patient Gift Packager
Silk Flower Arranger
Stenciling Service

Automotive

Auto Paint Touch-Up Professional
Auto Swap Meet Promotion
Automobile Window Stickers
Automotive Detailing

Business

Abstracting Service
Barter Systems
Business Plan Writer/Packager
Buyers Information Service
Consumer Researcher
Coupon Distributor
Direct Marketing/Sales
Efficiency Expert
Inventory Control
Lead Exchange/Business Networking
Multilevel Marketing
Rubber Stamp Business
Stenography Service
Telemarketing Service
Time Management Specialist
Word Processing Service

Computers

Bulletin Board Services
Internet Marketing Specialist
Scanning Service
Web Home Page Creator

Communication

Book Indexer
Clip Art Service
Clipping Service
Desktop Publisher: Community-Based
    Coupon Books
Freelance Writer/Editor/Illustrator
Handbill Distribution
In-Home Mail Service
Mailing List Service
Message Retrieval System/Answering
    Service
Public Relations

Education/Children

Child Care Referral Service
College Application Consultant
College Internship Placement
Day Care Service
Home Schooling Consultant
Parenting Specialist
Private Tutor

Employment Services

Athletic Recruiter/Scout
Career Counselor
On-Line Job Search
Resume Service
Secretarial Service

Entertainment/Arts
Band Manager
Color Consultant
Comedy Writer
Fan Club Management
Literary Agent
Movie Site Scout
Murder Mystery Producer

Environment
Commercial Plant-Watering Service

Financial Services
Bookkeeping Service
Credit Card Merchant Broker

Food/Beverage
Bartending Services
Cake Decorator
Caterer
Food Delivery Service
Herb Farming/Flowers
Herbal Products Distributor
Nutrition Consultant
Personal Menu Service
Taste Tester

Health Care
Childbirth Instructor
Doula/Midwife
Emergency Response Service
First Aid/CPR Instructor
Gerontology Consultant
Lactation Consultant
Medical Transcriptionist
Stress Management Counselor

Home Improvement
Fabric Coverings
Gardening Consultant
Interior Designer

Maid Service
Upholsterer

Miscellaneous
Graphologist
Parapsychologist
Reunion Organizer
Toy Cleaning Service

Personal Services
Bridal Consultant
Calendar Service
Calligrapher
Dance Instructor
Etiquette Advisor
Genealogical Service
Greeting Card Sender
Hospitality Service
Image Consultant
Knitting/Crochet Lessons
Laundry/Ironing Service
Lock Box Service
Makeup Artist
Manicurist
Massage Therapist
Mobile Hair Salon
Newspaper Delivery Service
Packing/Unpacking Service
Personal Instructor/Fitness Trainer
Personal Shopper
Personality Analysis/Testing Service
Professional Organizer
Referral Service
Reminder Service
Roommate Referral Service
Seamstress/Alterations

Pets & Animals
Horse Trainer
Pet Grooming/Care

Public Service/Legal

Adoption Search Service
Grants/Proposal Writer
Notary Public
Pollster
Workers' Compensation Consultant

Real Estate

Apartment Preparation Service
Traffic Control Consultant
Vacation Rentals Broker

Recreation

Arts Festival Promoter
Balloon Delivery Service
Bed & Breakfast
Entertainment Directory Publisher
Gift Basket Business
Magician

Party Planner
Recreational Coupon Distributor
Sales of Novelty/Promotional
   Products
Storyteller
Travel Agent

Transportation

Mobile Book/Magazine Distributor

Wholesale/Retail

Bridal Show Promotions
Catalog Retailer
Flea Market Organizer
Garage Sale Coordinator
Mall Promotion
Merchandise Demonstrator
Mystery Shopper
Rare Book Dealer/Search Service

Find more on this topic by visiting BusinessTown.com

Developed by Adams Media, **BusinessTown.com** is a free informational site for entrepreneurs, small business owners, and operators. It provides a comprehensive guide for planning, starting, growing, and managing a small business.

    Visitors may access hundreds of articles addressing dozens of business topics, participate in forums, as well as connect to additional resources around the Web. **BusinessTown.com** is easily navigated and provides assistance to small businesses and start-ups. The material covers beginning basic issues as well as the more advanced topics.

http://www.businesstown.com